JN288448

Conversations with God

Writings by **Toshu Fukami**

Copyright © 1999 by Toshu Fukami
All rights reserved

First Edition:First Impression   June 20, 2000
         Second Impression   June 20, 2002
         Third Impression   October 25, 2002
         Fourth Impression   January 20, 2013

Published by Tachibana Publishing Inc.

Tachibana Bldg.
2-20-9 Nishiogi-Minami
Suginami-ku, Tokyo 167-0053, Japan
Tel.(03)5941-2341
Fax.(03)5941-2348

Printed in Japan

Book design and Layout
by Sachiko Murakami
(Environmental Design Institute)
Photo:
amana images, IPJ, SEKAI BUNKA PHOTO,
ORION PRESS, KEYPHOTOS, JTB photo

Preface

This book is a collection of the favorite poems and inspirational writings of Toshu Fukami, a record of the spiritual journey of one of Japan's leading religious thinkers. Mr. Fukami is one of those rare individuals who believes there is no limitation to the potential of mankind, and he himself certainly embodies that in all that he does.

A successful businessman with a degree in economics from a prestigious private Japanese university, he is the CEO of a chain of successful ventures, including private-tutoring schools, a publishing firm, a trading company, and a travel agency. He also heads a management consulting firm and has written more than 270 books and recorded more than 220 lectures on topics such as business, self-improvement and confidence building that are available on CD and audio cassettes.

Mr. Fukami is also an accomplished artist in his own right. He is an opera singer, Noh actor, painter, calligrapher, composer, novelist, and poet who also writes haiku. He has received critical acclaim in all of these fields. Many of his musical and theatrical performances are available on CD and DVD, and his calligraphy and paintings have been widely published. He regularly organizes charity events for humanitarian causes.

This book, the first in a series called Conversations with God, is a record of Mr. Fukami's spiritual journey. Strongly influenced by Shinto—Japan's most popular religion—Mr. Fukami has worked for years to prove its value as a living faith based on tolerance and self-growth, which can be applied effectively to both business and one's own personal life. The Conversations with God series is an ongoing record of Mr. Fukami's encounter with this delicate and refined world of culture, art, creativity, and beauty, and it serves as a welcome guide for anyone wishing to embark on a path of self-improvement or personal growth.

To greet each and every morning with prayer.
It seems to be effortless
And yet few tasks are more difficult.

No prayer goes unheard;
No prayer goes unanswered.
The more voices gathered together in prayer,
The quicker God responds.

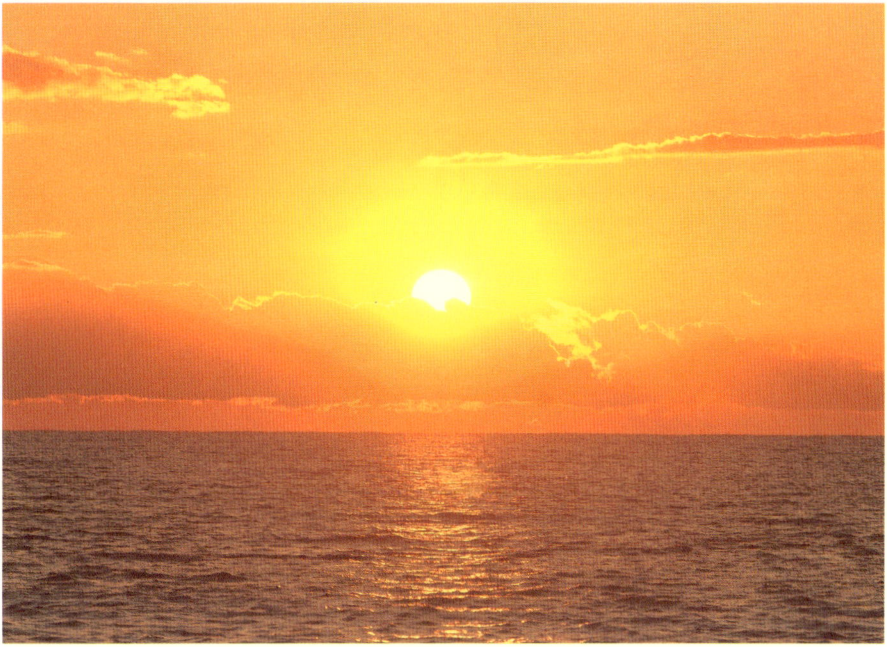

When one looks at a mountain
So beautiful that words fail,
One enters the Sixth Realm,
The seat of the feelings of the soul.

Sixth Realm
Consisting of free-form poetry, this book conveys the search for the highest spiritual realm which the intellect can perceive, the stage known as the 'Sixth Realm'.
As described metaphorically by Mr.Fukami, the dimensions progress from the realm in which we live, the third dimension, to the realm or spirits, the fourth dimension. Beyond that is a realm inhabited by the known deities, the Fifth Realm.
Above even this lies the Sixth realm. Images of this realm are manifested by great flashes of artistic inspiration or in intuitions of unparalleled creativity and beauty.

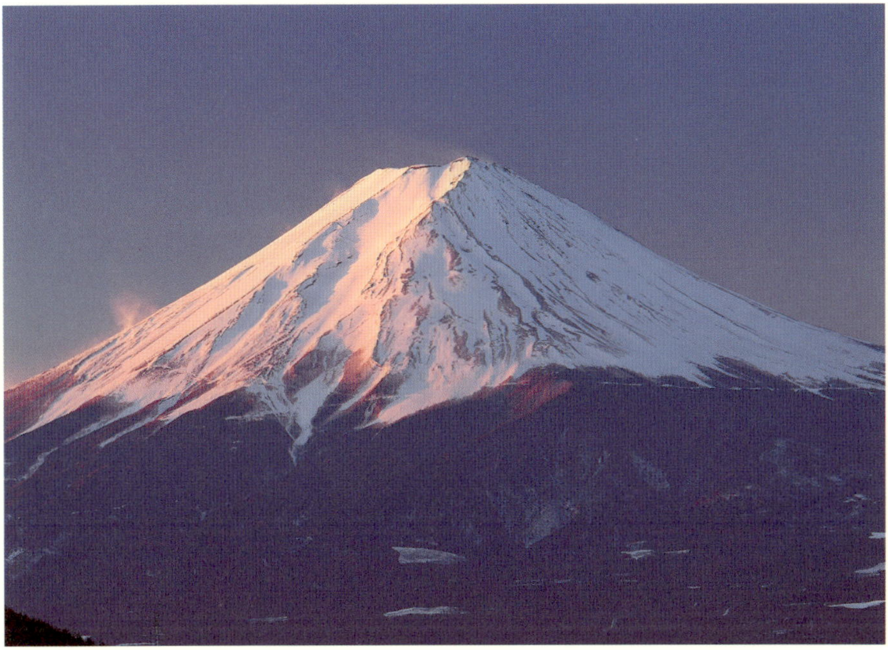

From heat, comes cold.
Only when the heart is cold,
Can something which will warm it be born.
This is one of the mysteries
Of the evolution of the Heavens
To be understood only by those of refined spirit.

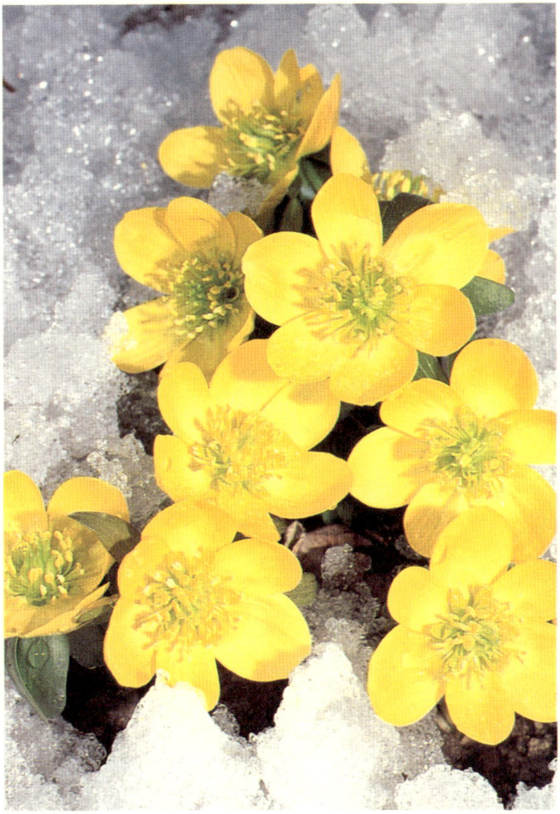

The bird does not worry about material things
A flower in bloom does not question people
Even when it may be snapped from its branch,
It voices no complaint.
The flower and the singing birds
Know of nothing but bringing happiness to Man.
Surely these are manifestations of God in His greatness.

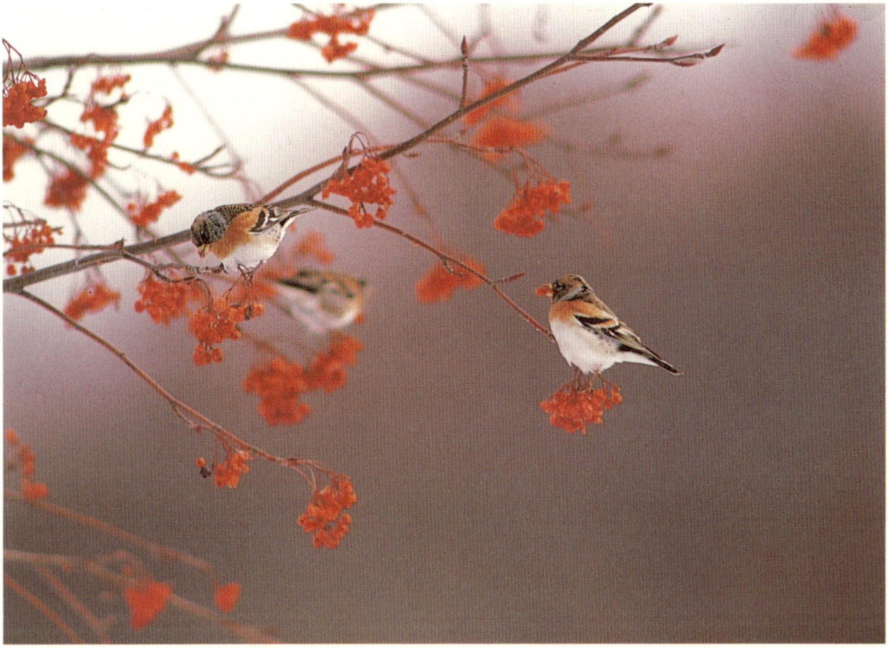

If you truly desire to speak with God,
Speak to a songbird.
If you truly wish to see God,
Behold the glory of the mountains,
The ocean, the flowers in bloom
There you shall see Him.

If, still, you say that you have not experienced God,
Then trust someone unconditionally
And love them with all your heart.
The spirit of true love
Is not far from the heart of God.

God is not something to be known,
But something to be felt.
He only needs to be loved.
Love is the most basic relationship between God and man.

The love between two people,
The love between mother and child,
Both furnish a glimpse of the love which is God.

The burning, the desire,
The longing for a home only distantly remembered
All are but pale memories
Of the Spirit which has dwelt within man
Since he became flesh.

This spirit is a legacy from time immemorial
Lying within the human heart.
The True Mind of those determined
To search for the Sixth Realm.

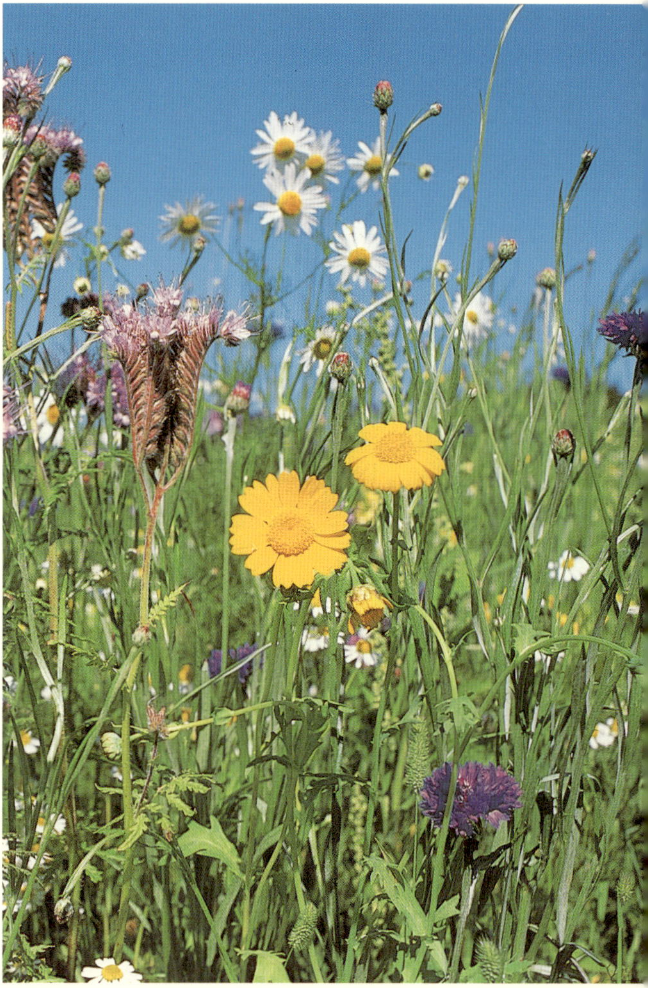

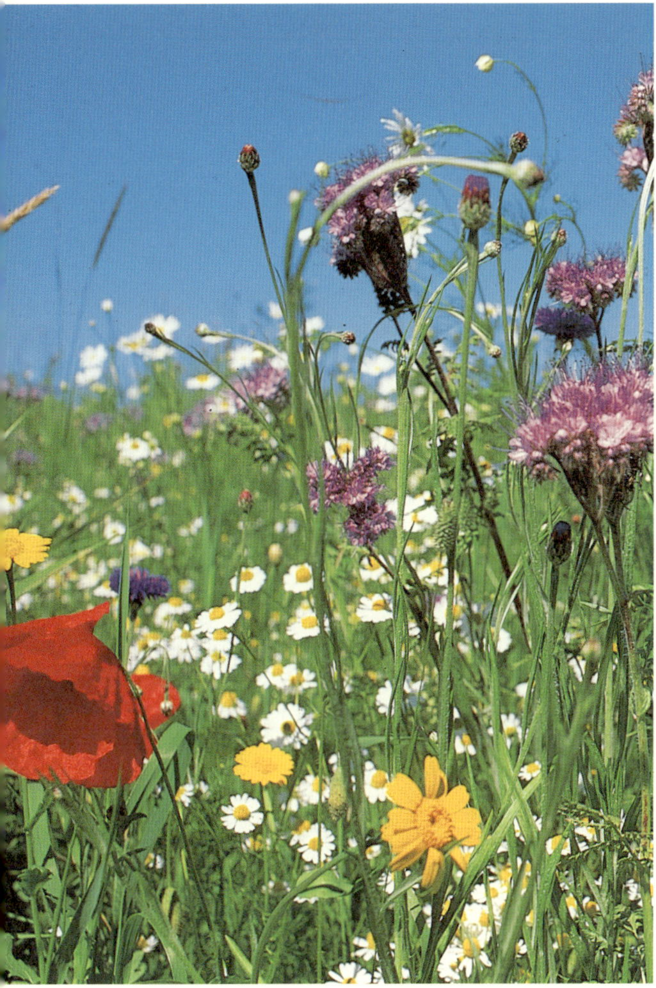

What pleases Man pleases God.
God does not dwell in some far off place,
God is present in the everyday world.

The chains of the world of man
Are products of Man's actions
And not the vengeance of a wrathful God.

Do not be afraid,
For God dwells within each and every one of us.
Realize this truth and
Your troubles, your fears, your anxieties
Fade into calm.

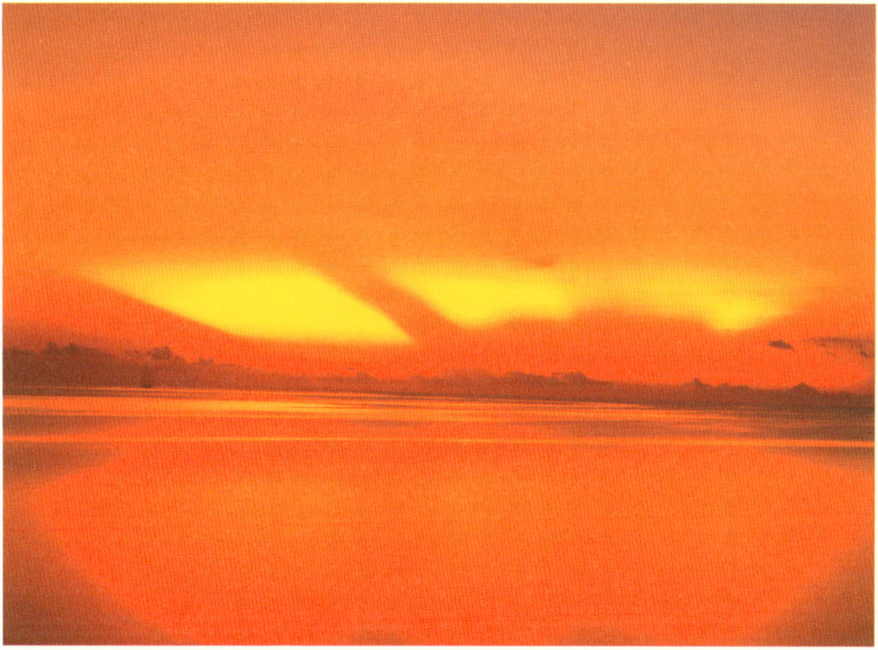

Man is God made flesh.
Man is the very breath of God.
Man is the very heart of God.

Witness, within your own heart, the history of humanity.
Powerful hints for the path are to be found there.
There lies the heart and teaching of God,
Revealed in His form and actions.

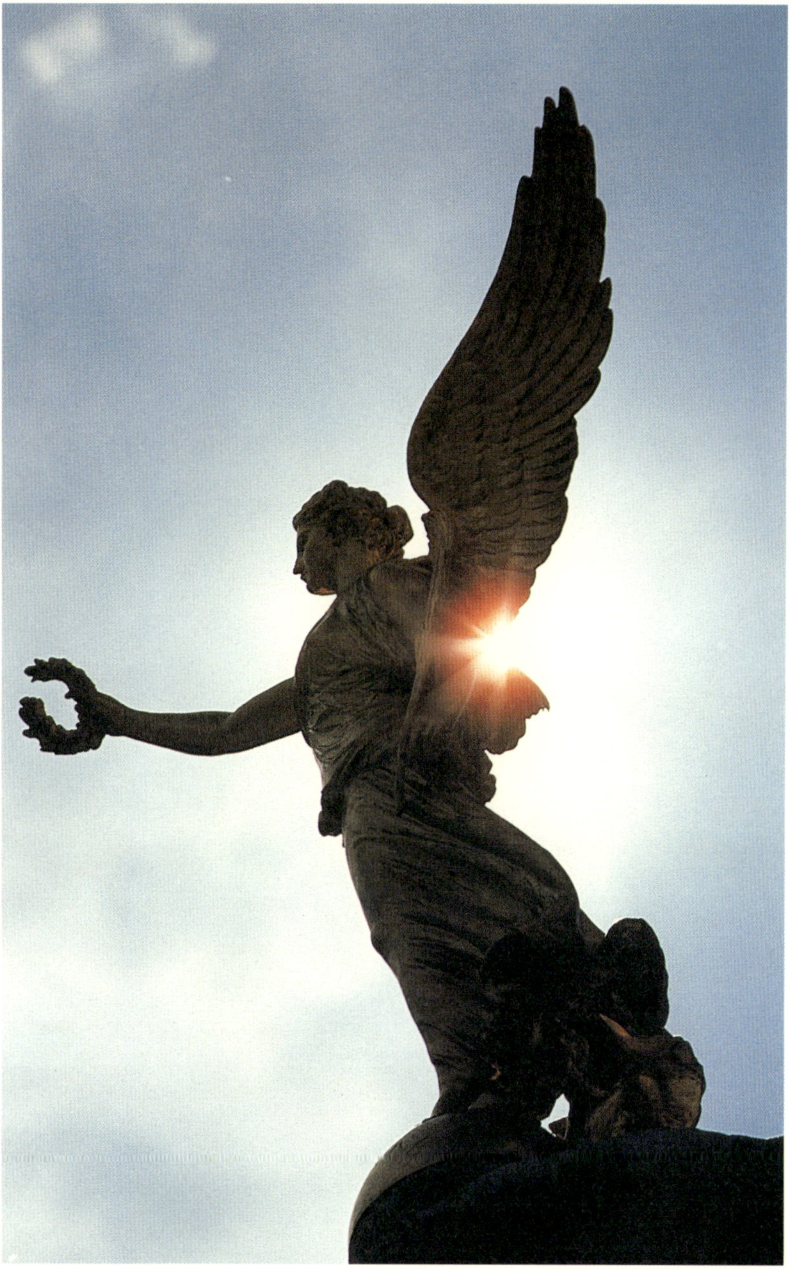

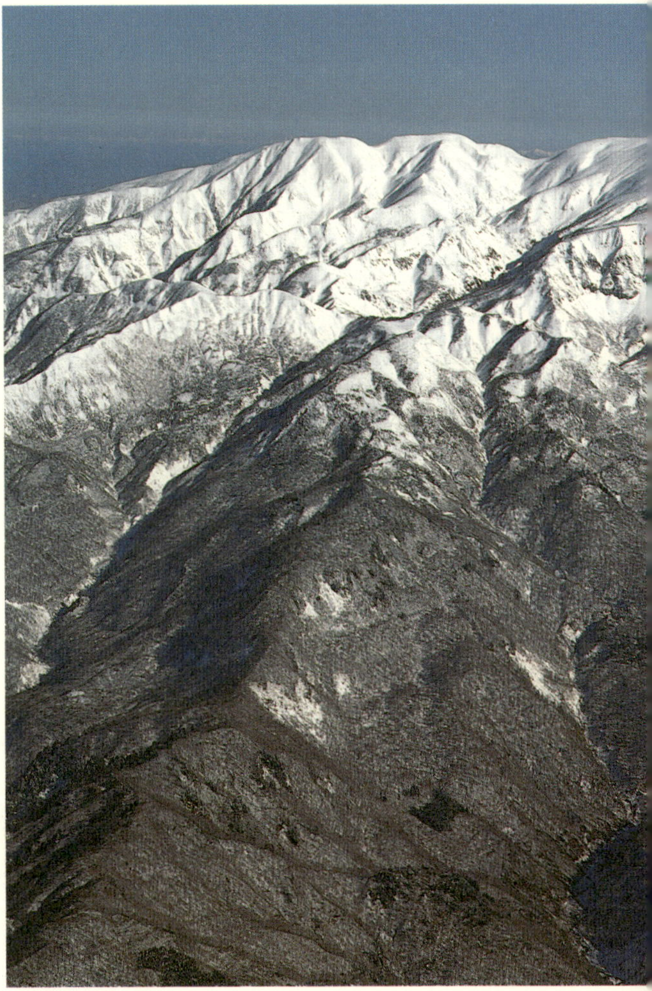

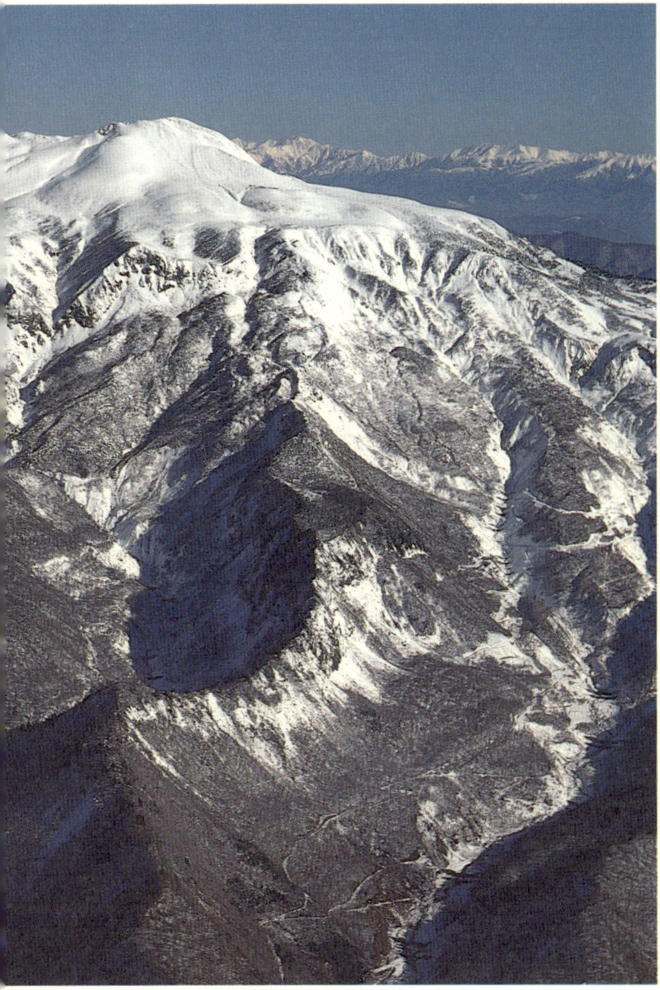

If you wish to know what Man is,
Turn your gaze towards history.

Study what people have done in the past.
Anything accomplished by someone in the past
You can do
If you set your mind to it.

Discern what is old in that which is new.
Discern what is new in that which is old.
This is your enlightenment.

Things of antiquity teach the Way
Things which are new delight the senses.
Being able to blend the old and the new
Is the sign of a wise man who has grasped truth in its totality.
There is nothing under the heavens beyond his grasp.

Almost all profound knowledge and insight
Is discovered after closely reading the great writers.
Make their study your first goal on the way to self-perfection.

If after reading the Great Books,
No insights surface,
Do not be dismayed, the time is not yet right.

The Great Books are models of beautiful prose and clarity of thought
They bring understanding to every serious reader
Who is willing to accept the challenge of studying them.

What fitting monuments,
These books,
To the great lives of the men and women who wrote them.

DANCE and SKYLARK
JOHN MOORE

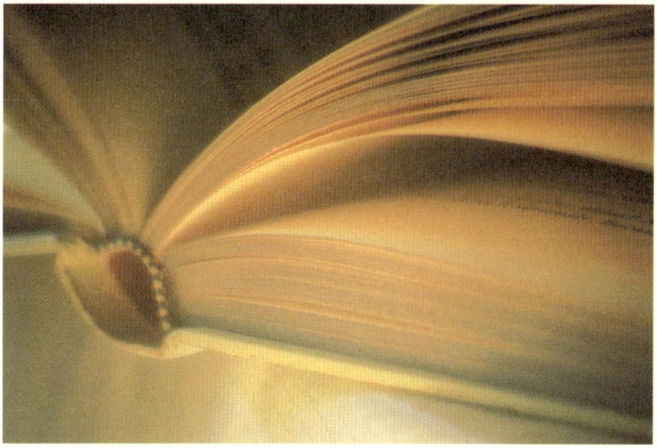

It is only after repeating countless practice studies
That an artist is finally able to tackle a great masterpiece.
Do not begrudge the effort required
Before you begin any undertaking.

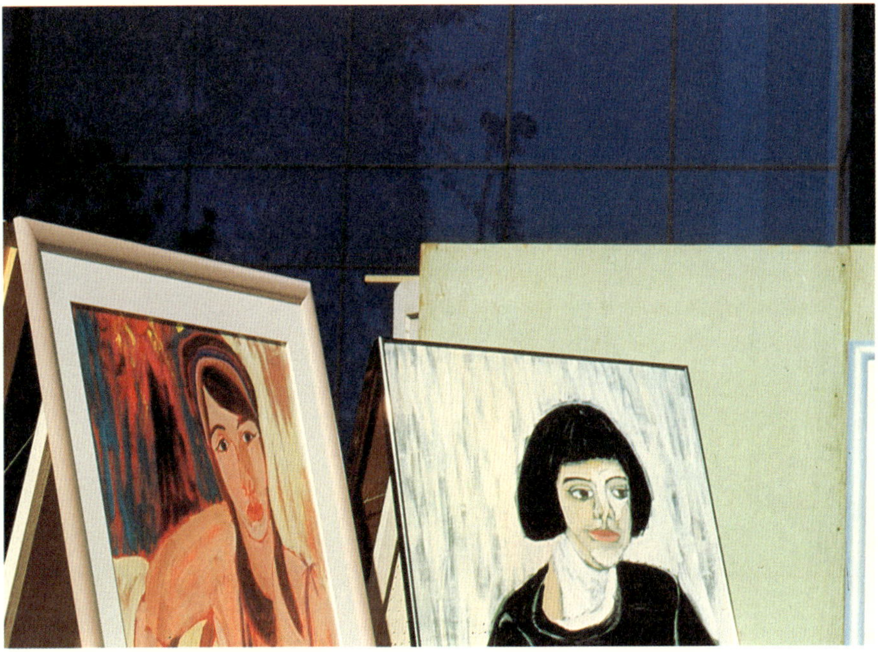

Do not worry.
At any point in your life,
There is still ample time
To study and sharpen your mind.
The tragedy is that most people
Go throughout life without realizing this.

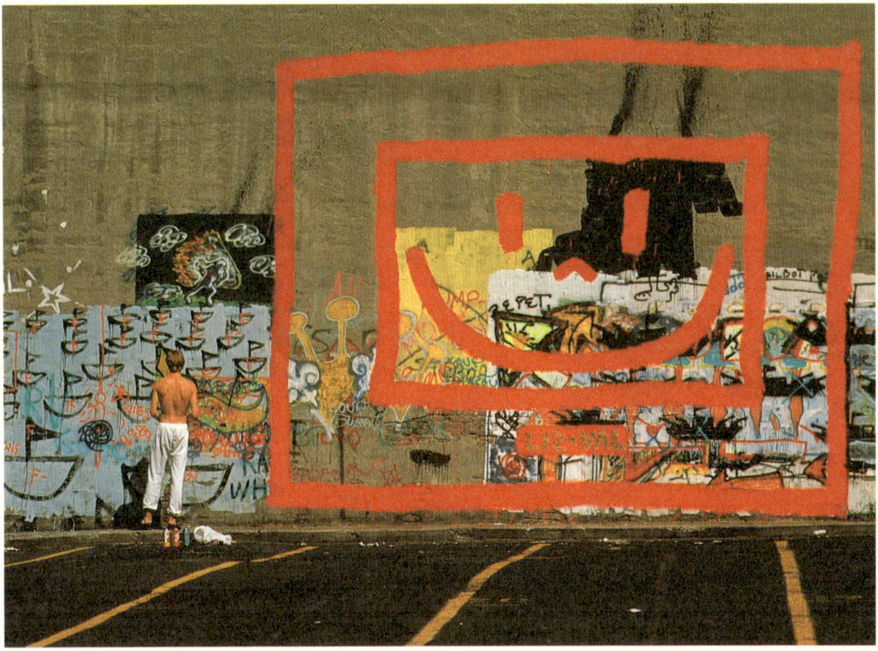

The beginning of progress in studies
Is clearly discerning the difference between
What you know and what you do not know.
Only a person with humility
Can see themselves as they truly are.

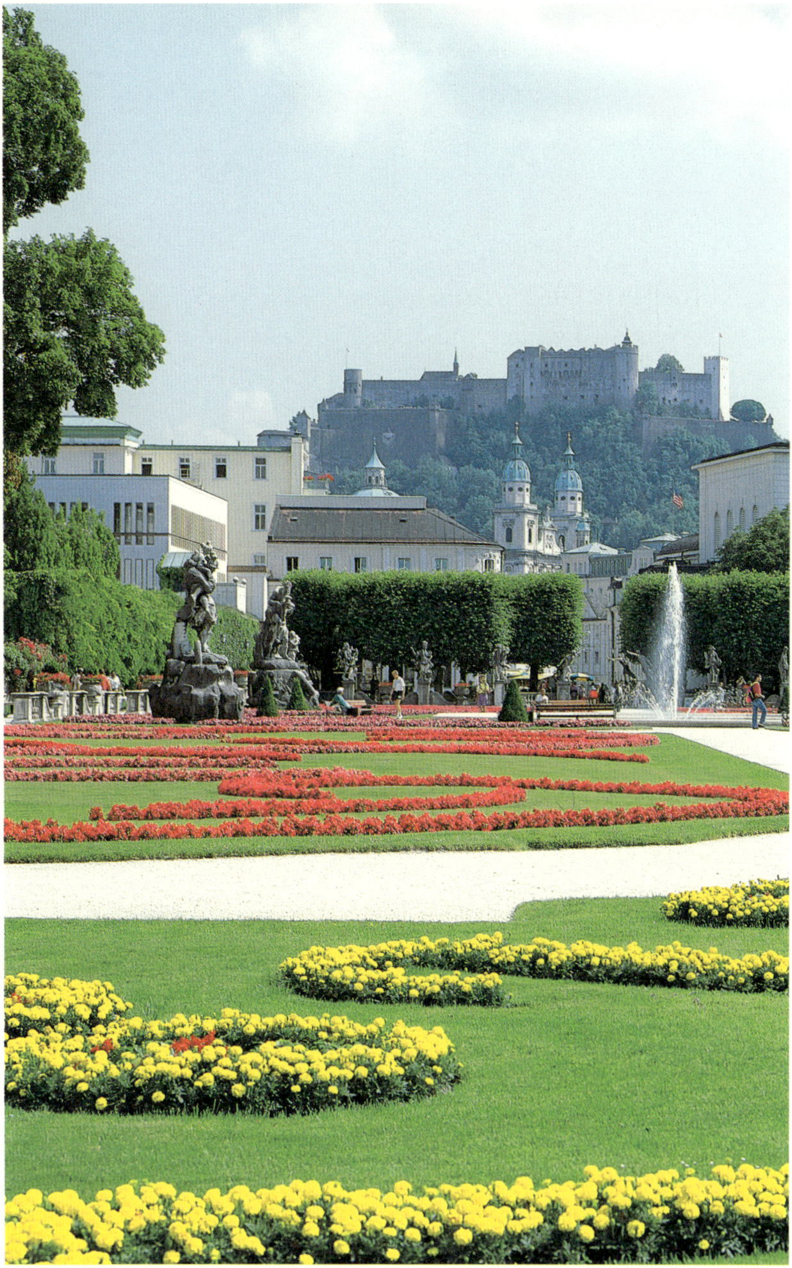

Coming to know that which once you did not know
That alone is enough to greatly advance the soul.

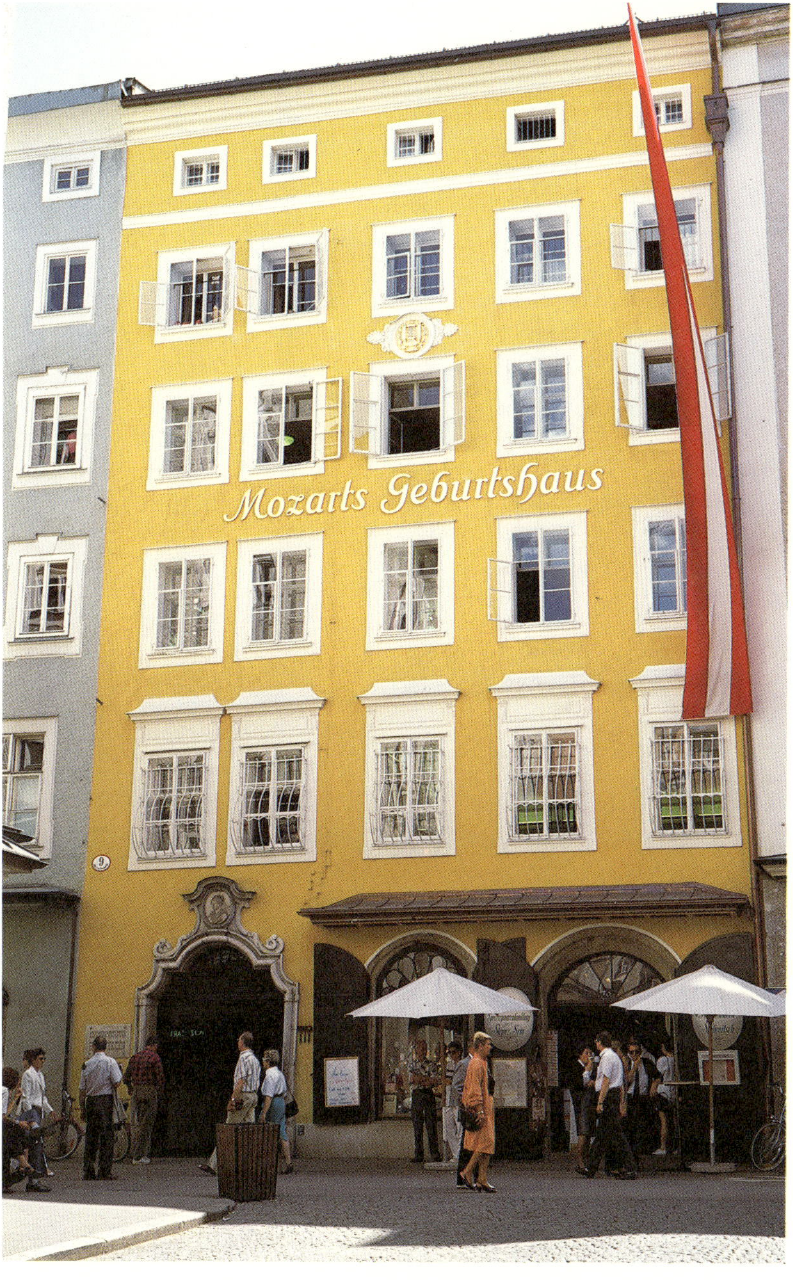
Mozarts Geburtshaus

Reaching the stage
Where you yearn to understand more
That alone is enough to be considered
Progress along the path to self-growth.

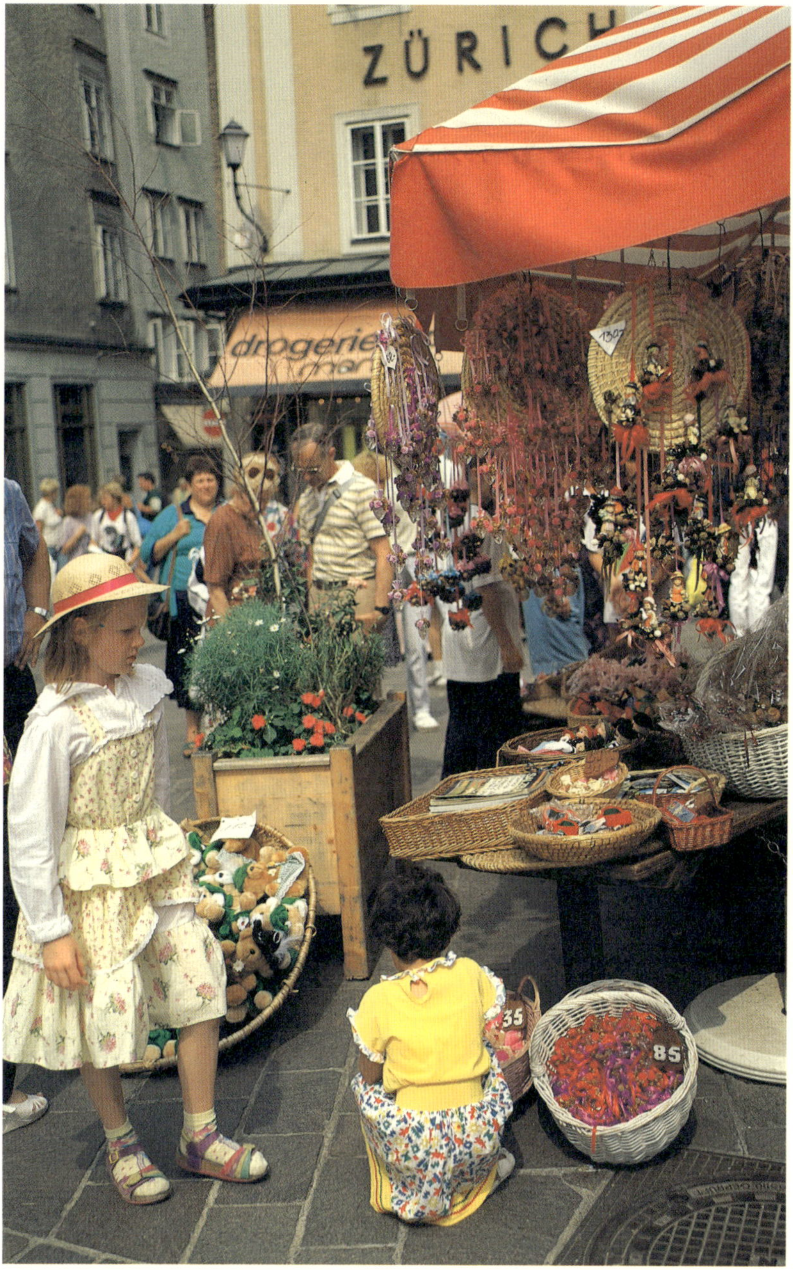
ZÜRICH
drogerie

To want to improve yourself
So you many become a truly outstanding individual
That alone is necessary
To start you on the path
To becoming one with God.

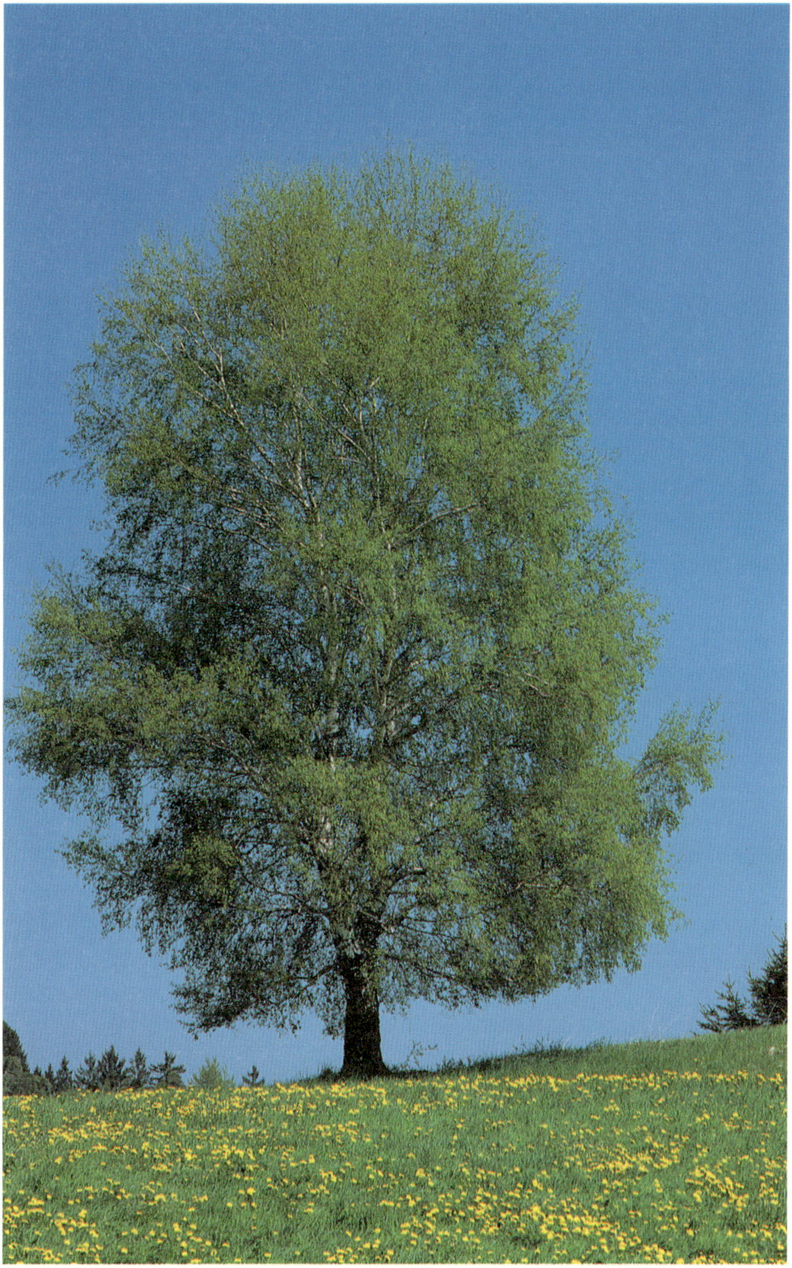

What is enlightenment?
It is determination.
The living and those who have passed away
Who cannot become enlightened as to the Path
Those who cannot wake up to the Will of Heaven
Fail to do so because they lack determination.

Who has the greatest determination?
Those who are willing to abandon the self.

Most people are bound to the notion of the small self.
And thus deny themselves progress
Towards compassion and cooperation,
Towards purification which would render
Their spirit as pure as crystal in water.

Realize that the self is nothing more than the smallest part of the soul
Because it is the smallest part of the soul,
People become obstinate.
Because it is the smallest part of the soul,
Whenever it becomes necessary
To view a situation from a larger vantage,
This small self cannot resist asserting itself.

The Greater Soul is accepting and tolerant of others.
When you forget the self, forget it completely.
Only when the soul is freed from the self,
Will you be able to manifest
The highest values in both your spirit and your life.

Break free from self-complacent living,
Stop being satisfied
With a pale glimpse of the smallest enlightenment.
Without enlightenment, faith and prayer mean nothing.
Without enlightenment,
There can be no progress or development.
Where there are neither progress nor development,
Life is barren, devoid of all meaning.

Choose
What it is you seek to become enlightened to?
What it is you are determined to accomplish?
DecideThe time has come.

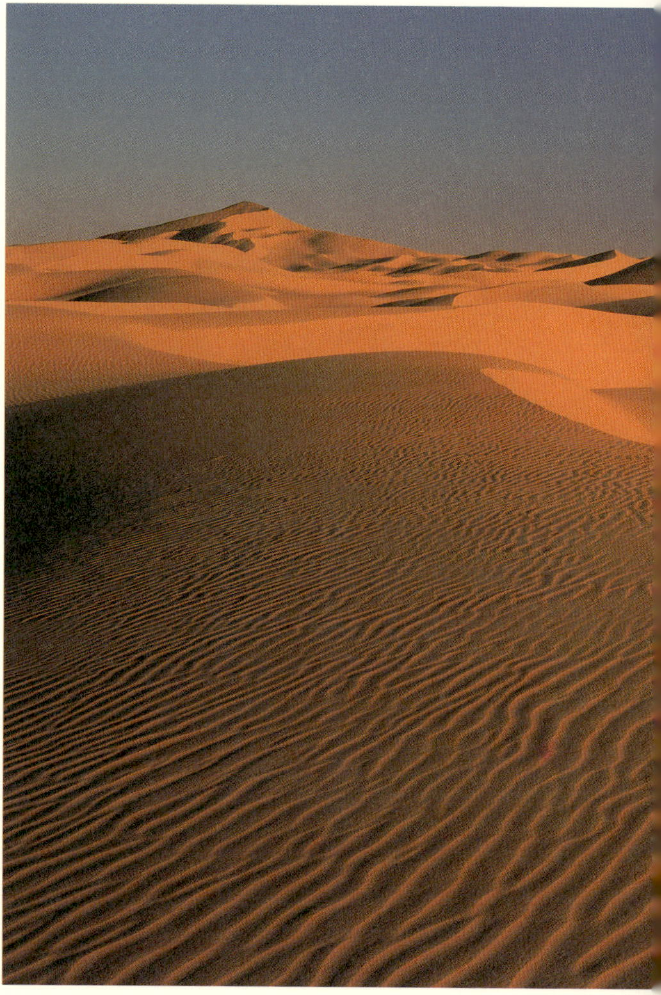

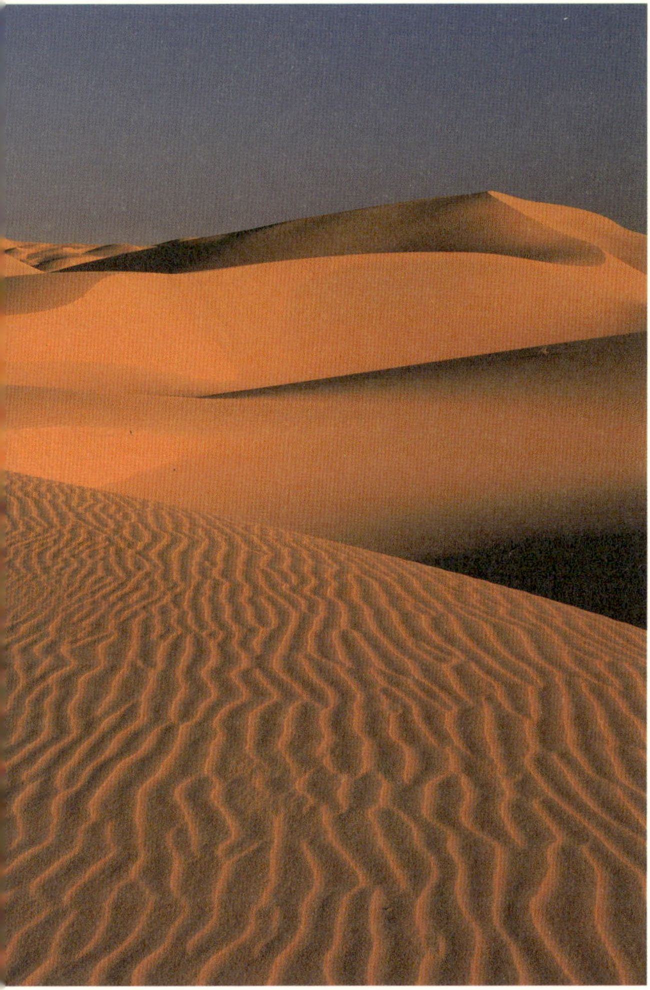

As they grow old,
Some people loose their passion for life.

Even if they are spiritually inclined,
They cannot be said to be people
Who dwell in the presence of God's love
Because God's true love manifests itself
By embracing life to the fullest.

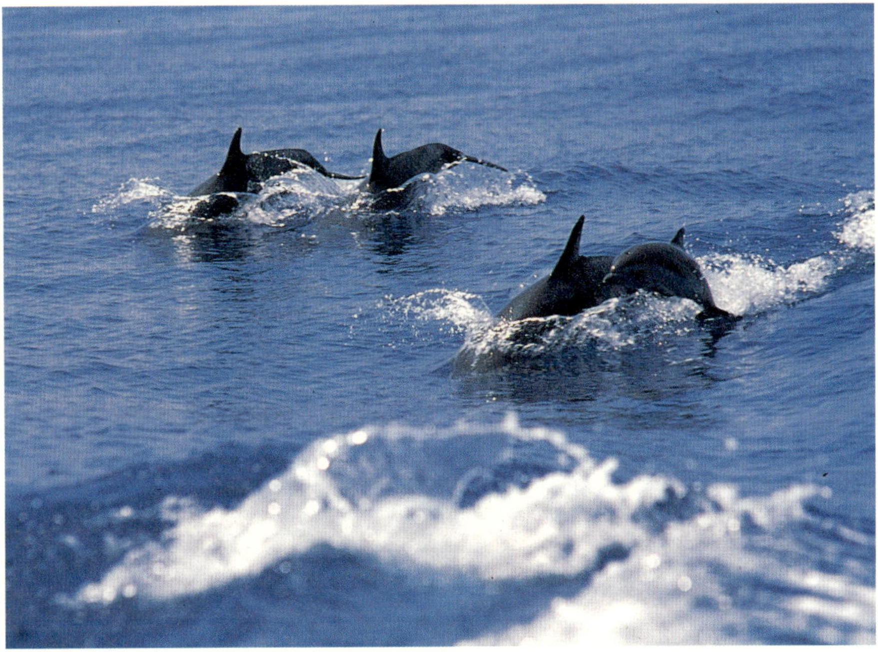

Growing old is caused
By a loss of the spirit of adventure.
The moment you loose your spirit of adventure,
You begin to grow old.
Health and physical strength are
The fruits of will and spiritual strength.
Will and spiritual strength are born from a spirit of adventure.

Accept challenges, embrace adventure.
Discover and embrace the courage within.
What really is to be feared
Is when the heart withers and grows old.
The spirit itself looses its brightness.
The soul itself begins a backwards slide.
Only if you grasp the purpose for which you were born,
Will you be able to embrace the challenges of life.

Adventure comes from challenging the unknown.
It overcomes the doubting mind
Which sees only the impossible,
It conquers the calculating mind
Which sees only the effort which will be required.

Adventure is the working of the power of the soul.
The purpose of life is to further develop our souls
Through each incarnation.

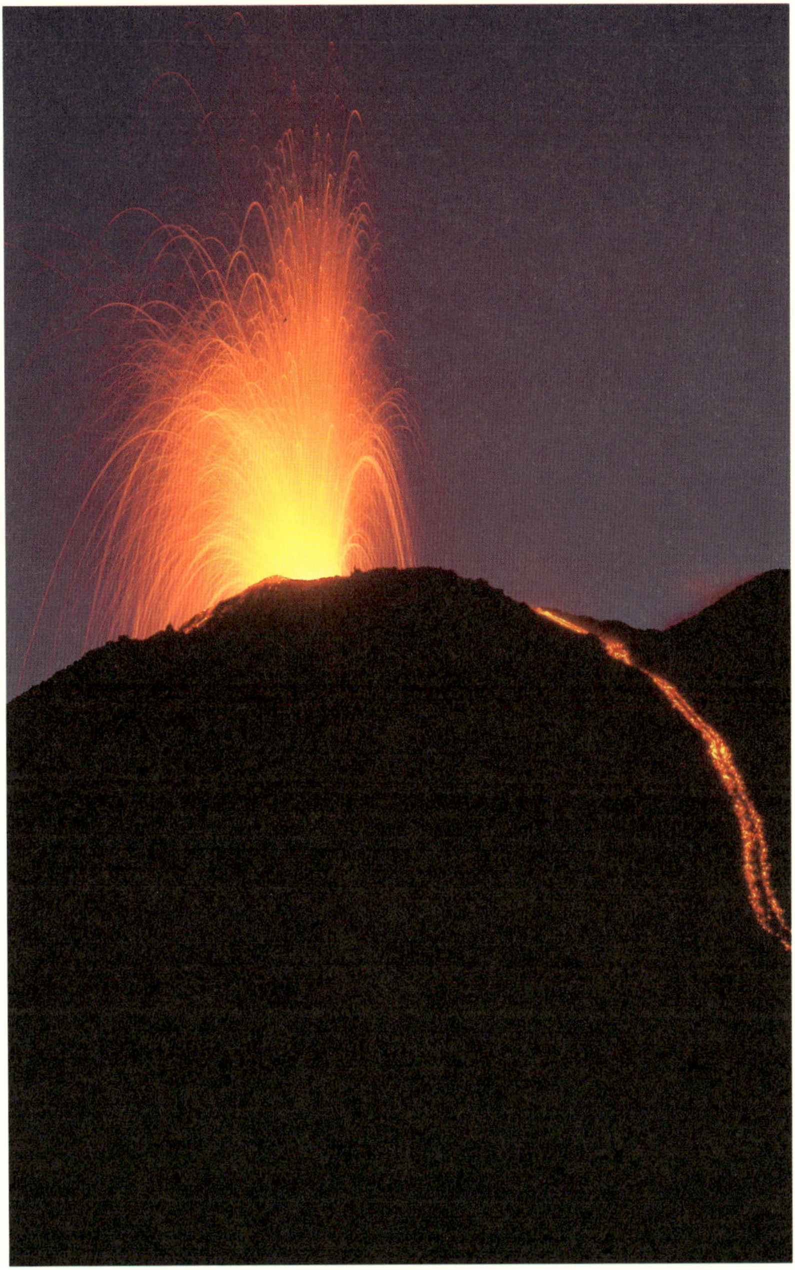

It is said that acceptance of life as it is
Is one of the graces given to people at the close of their lives.

Until then, be aggressive and brave.
Be unafraid to seek out the spritual challenges you need for growth.

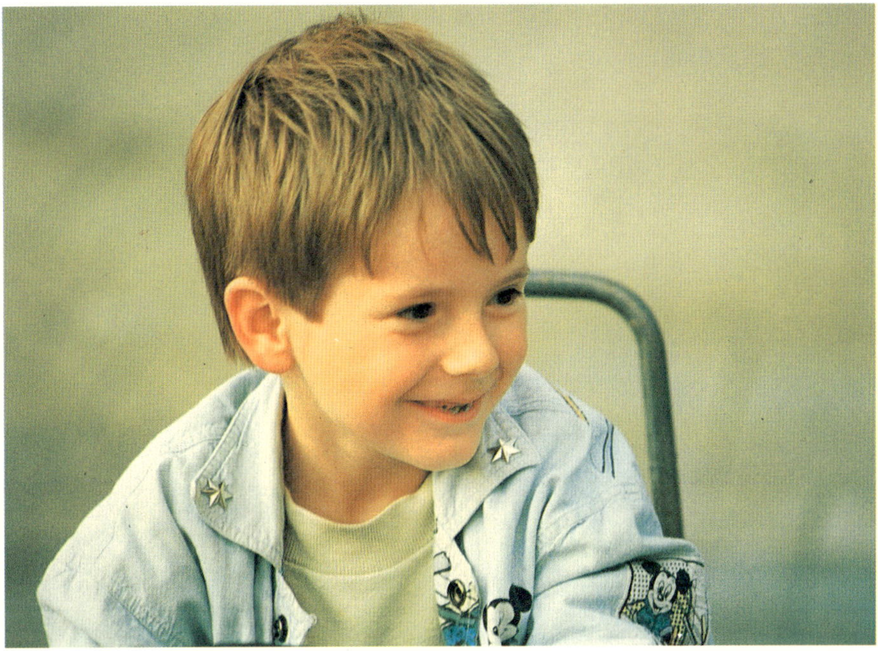

Centering the mind cannot be done by sitting in the idle meditation

Truth is reached by polishing the soul
Through the challenges of everyday life,
Through the magnificence and mystery of art.

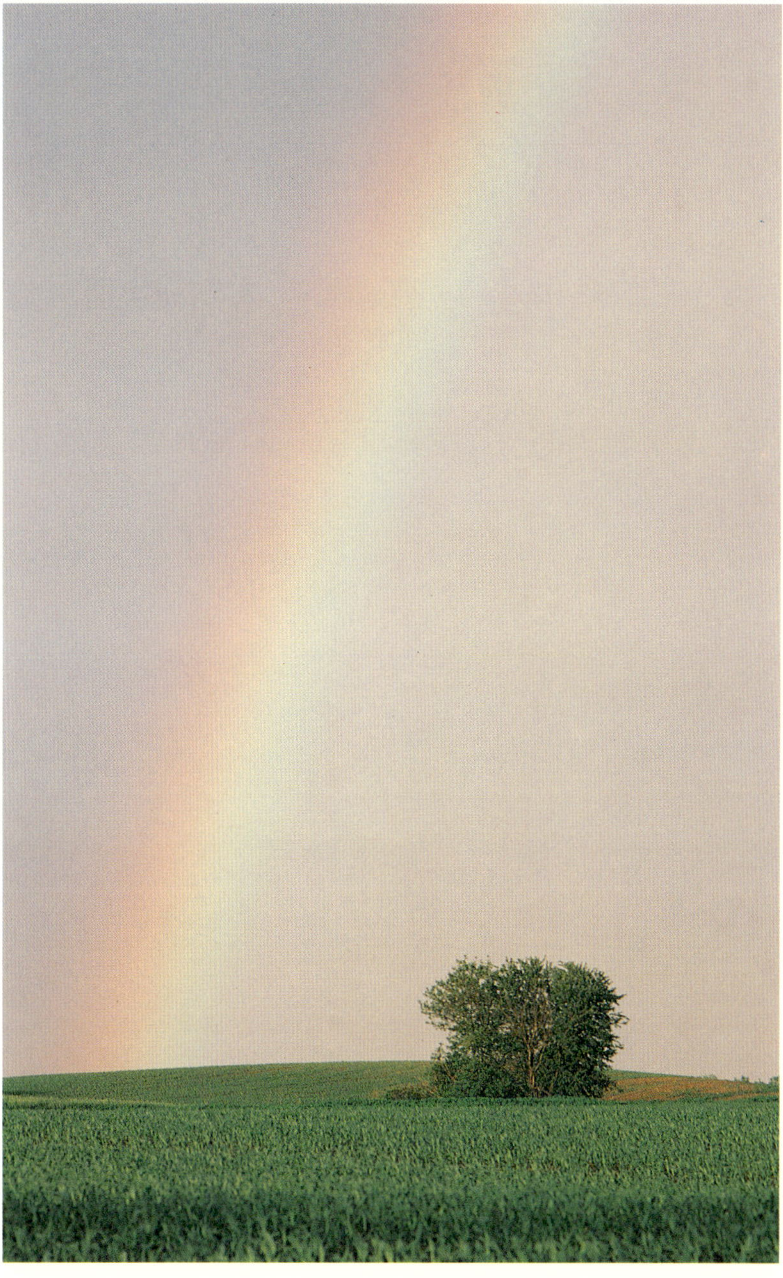

Accept everything positively and optimistically.
Aggressively search for things to thank God for.

Spiritual practice in everyday life
Consists of practicing a new way of viewing life.

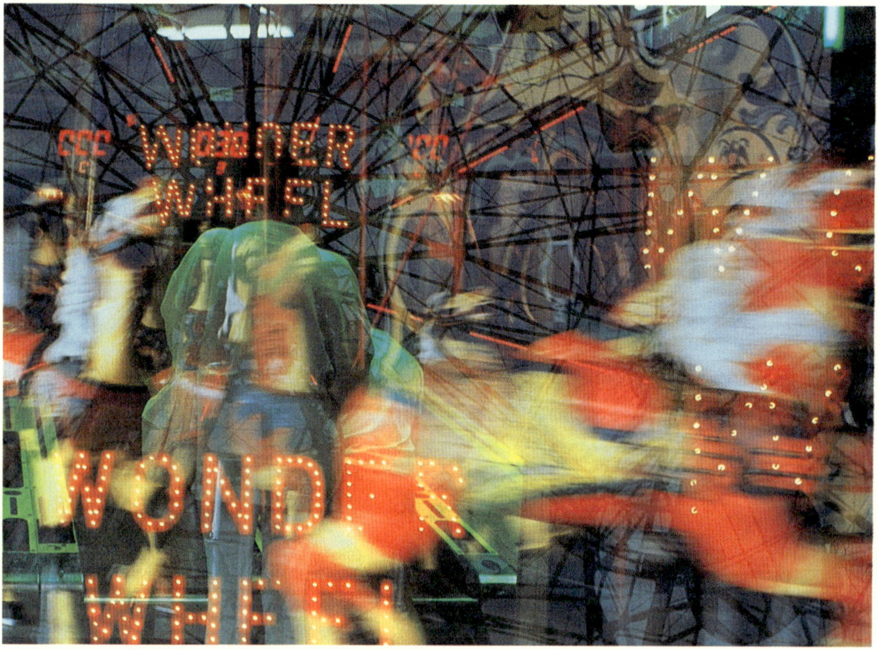

All of the answers for which you might ask
All of the guidance of which you might dream
Are right before your very eyes.

Discoveries are not necessarily made
At the exact moment when you are looking for them.

God sees your yearning for knowledge and
Sends the grace needed for understanding.

This is what religious seekers in the East have called
'Wisdom beyond imagination'.

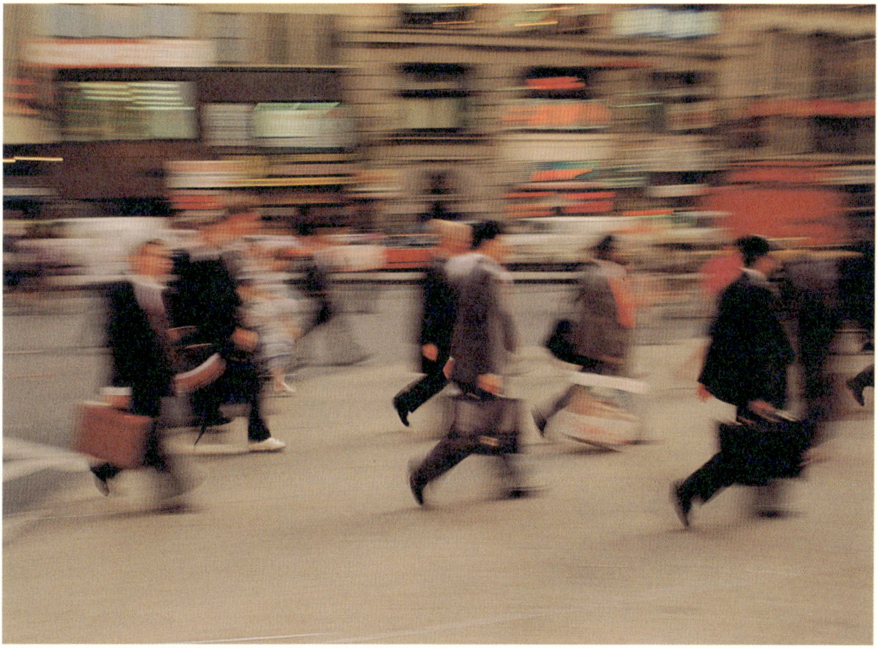

Words which do not come from within,
Cannot be said to be words from the heart.

Words resonating with truth
Are always words which tell
Of that which you have experienced yourself
And thus are a part of your very being.

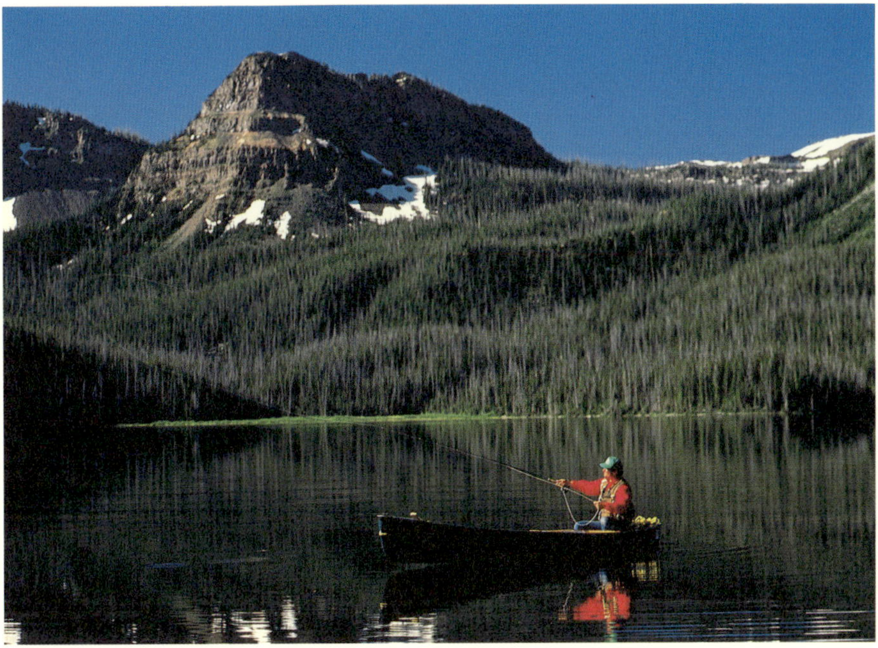

Cherish the ordinary mind.
Make right your conduct,
Make right your speech.
Your heart should always shine
With the brightness of sun and the splendor of moon.

When dealing with people,
Display a thoughtfulness as gentle as soft moonlight.

Sometimes,
To make the calm moon even more placid,
God calls forth storms
And intersperses his admonitions with thunder and rain.

The mists clouding the moon at dawn,
Are quickly brushed away by the God of Wind
In preparation for daybreak.

Like this,
Relationships between people mirror
The beauty and rhythms of nature.

By knowing the old,
We can make ourselves new
With each dawning day.

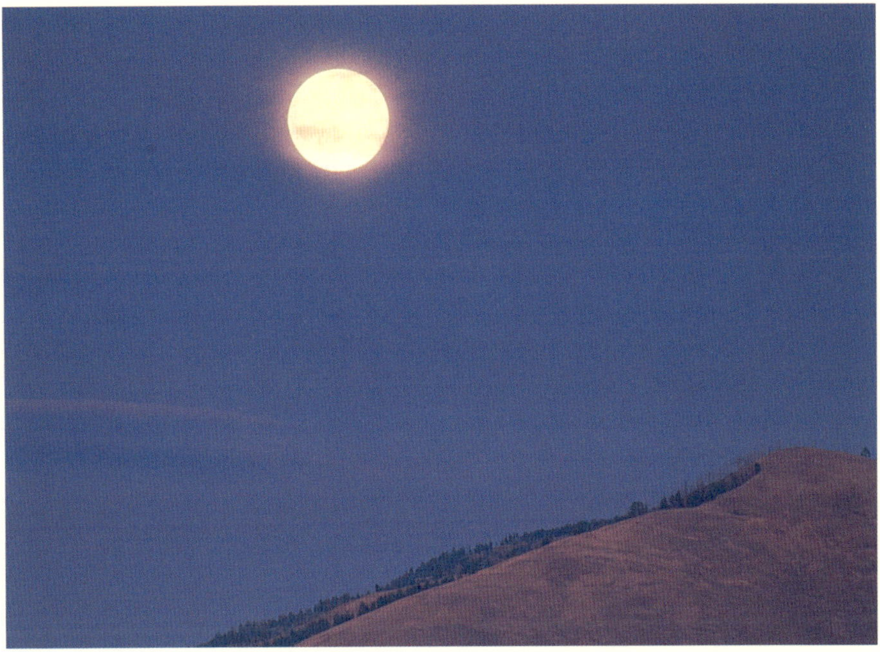

Some say that God does not give two gifts to one person.
Others claim that people's lives are fixed
By an immutable destiny
From the moment of birth.

In reality,
It is simply that those aspects
Developed in previous lives
Bear the fruits of fortune in this one.

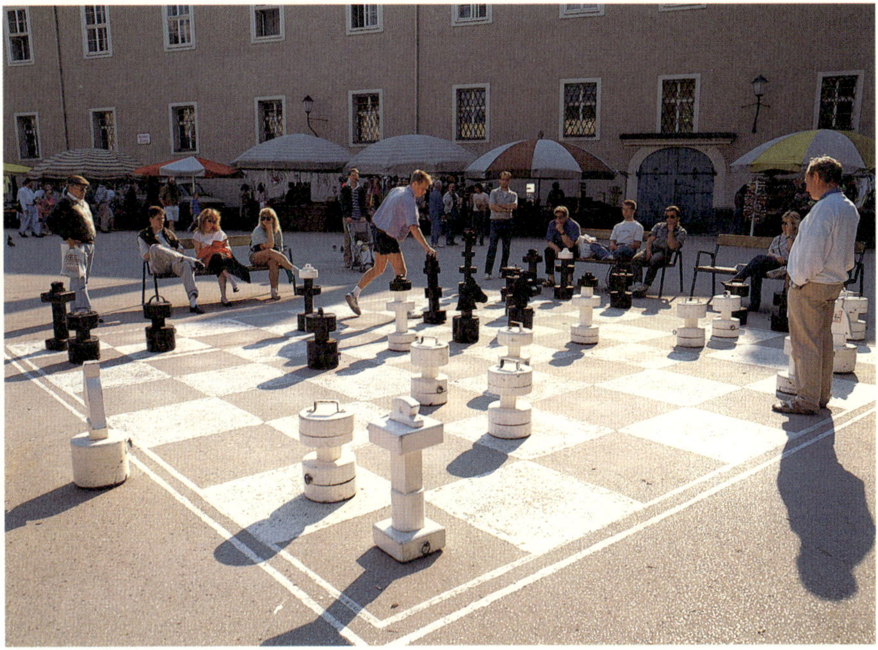

Do not scorn others.
Everyone carries different burdens from past lives.

If people strive in this life,
They will receive rewards in proportion to their efforts,
Rewards which they will carry on to their next life.

Three things have the potential to carry over into the next life

Faith and an inclination toward the spiritual path,
Artistic talents and sensitivity,
Knowledge achieved through study and learning.

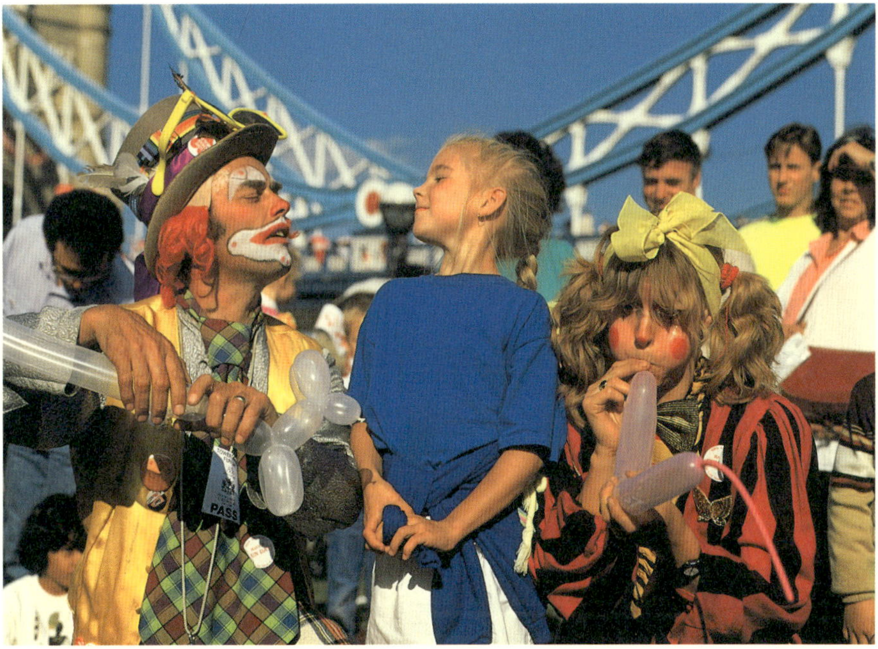
PASS

What is freedom?
Freedom is the flexibility and loftiness of character
Which allows you to deal pleasantly and enjoyably
With people from all walks of life.

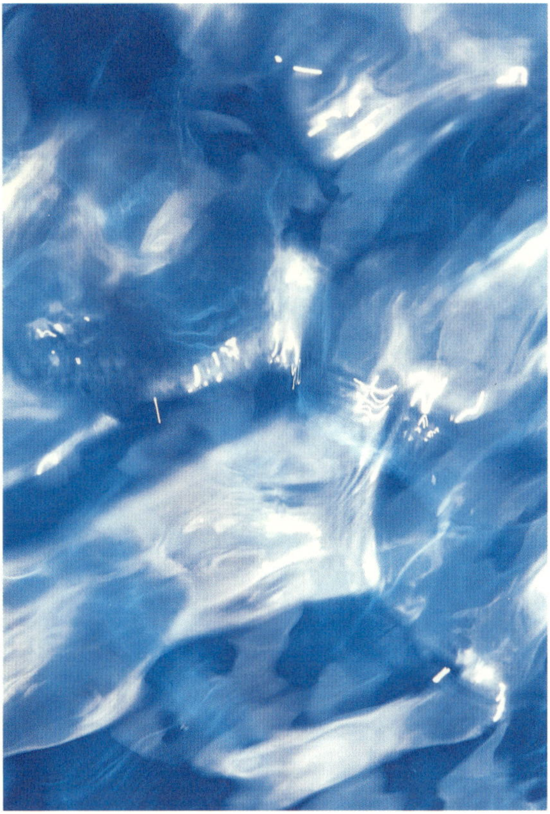

Many people find themselves
Unable to let go of the past.
Even after they have done all which was possible.

Even more are the number of people
Who mourn dreams which linger unfulfilled.

These people do so because they have not abandoned their selves,
And have not become Love itself.

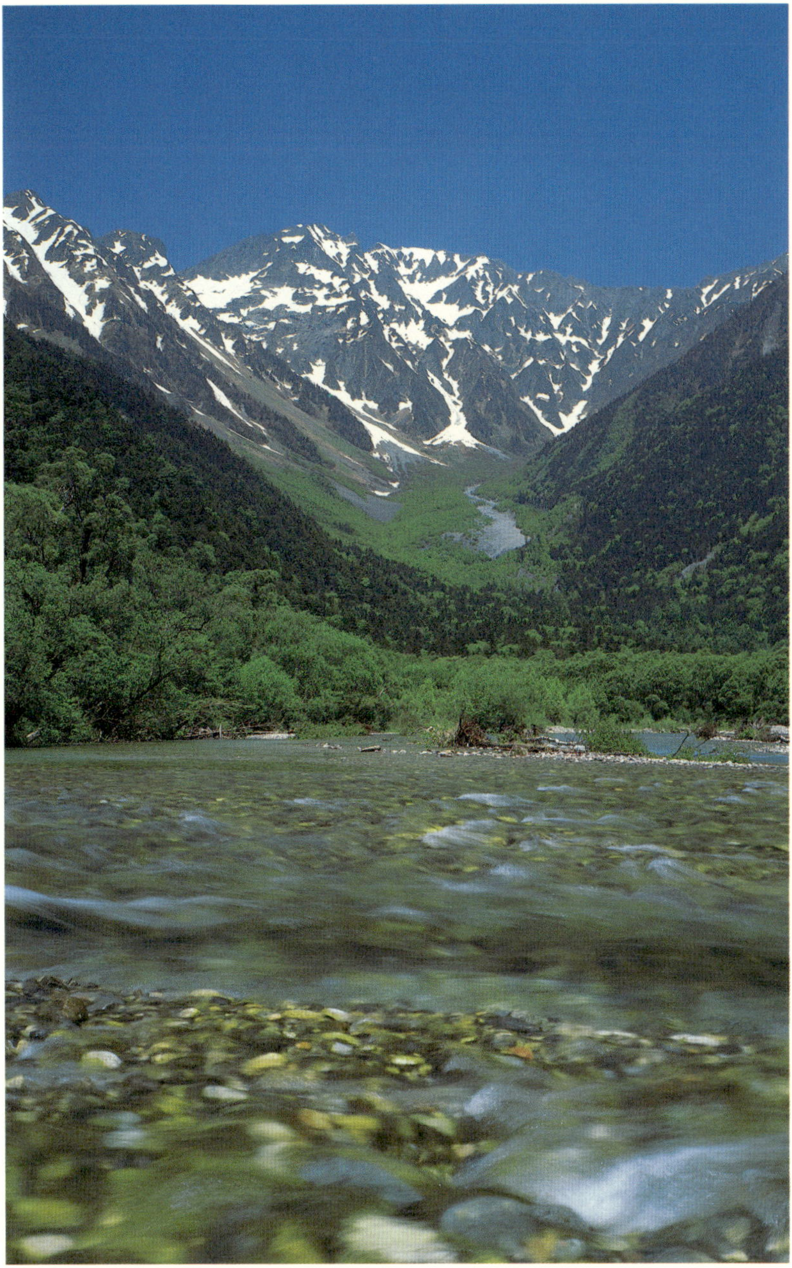

Although you may face adversity,
As people who live in the very presence of God
Believe that all will turn out for the best.
No matter what may confront you.

For this is the way God looks out for His people.

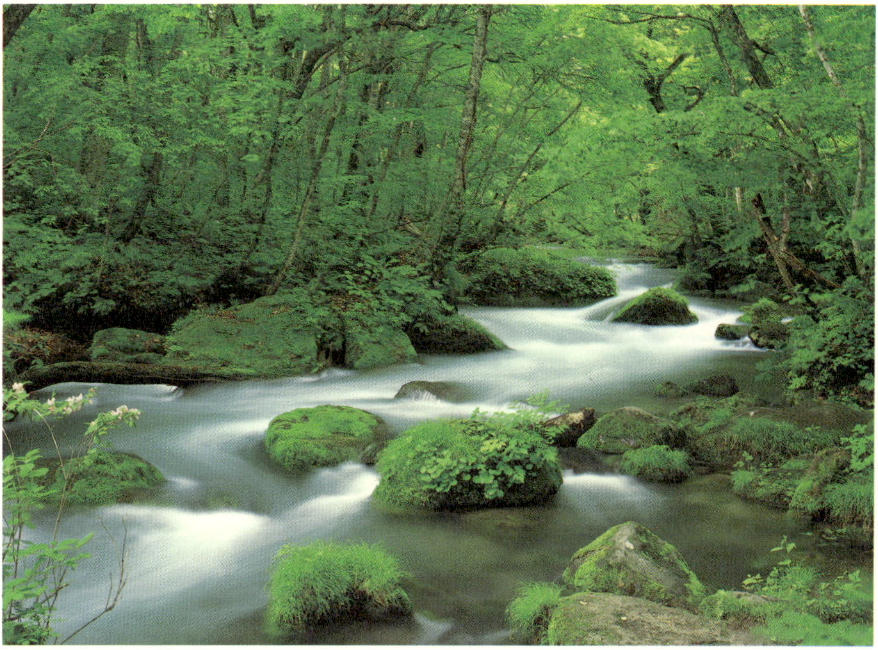

Impatience is the root of all troubles.
Hateful words, thoughtless actions, loss of harmony
All stem from being impatient.

A saying has it that a gem will not shine unless it is polished.
But how should it be polished and in which way?
If you simply grind away, it will be reduced to worthless dust.

In polishing a gem,
It is crucial to know
When to go fast and when to go slow,
When to be strong and when to be gentle.

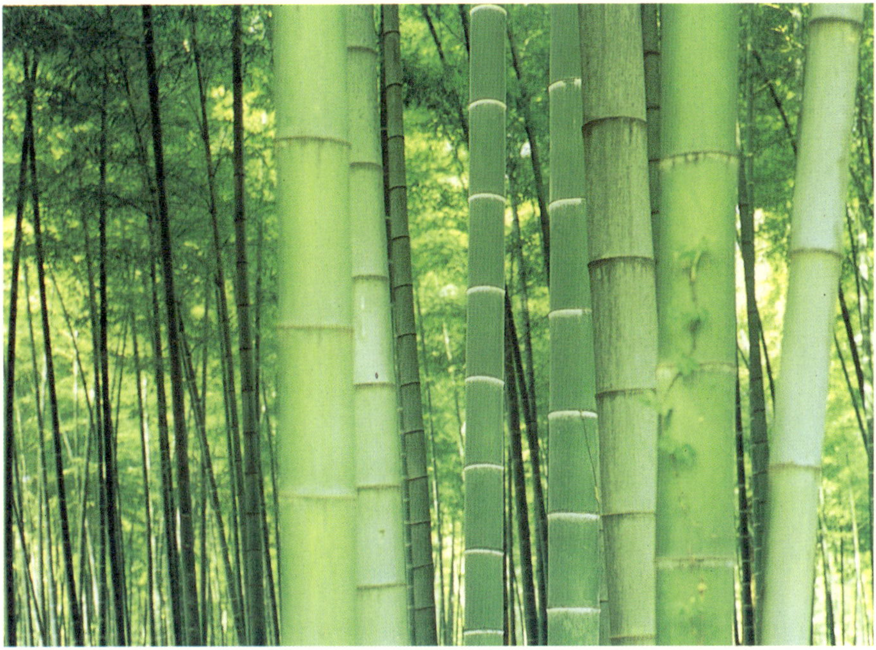

Those who see good and evil,
Who know the difference between right and wrong
And yet do nothing
Seek peace at the price of justice.

Keeping things in proper order,
Bringing things into harmony is most important.
It is in structuring the world around you
That you gain the discipline to structure the mind.

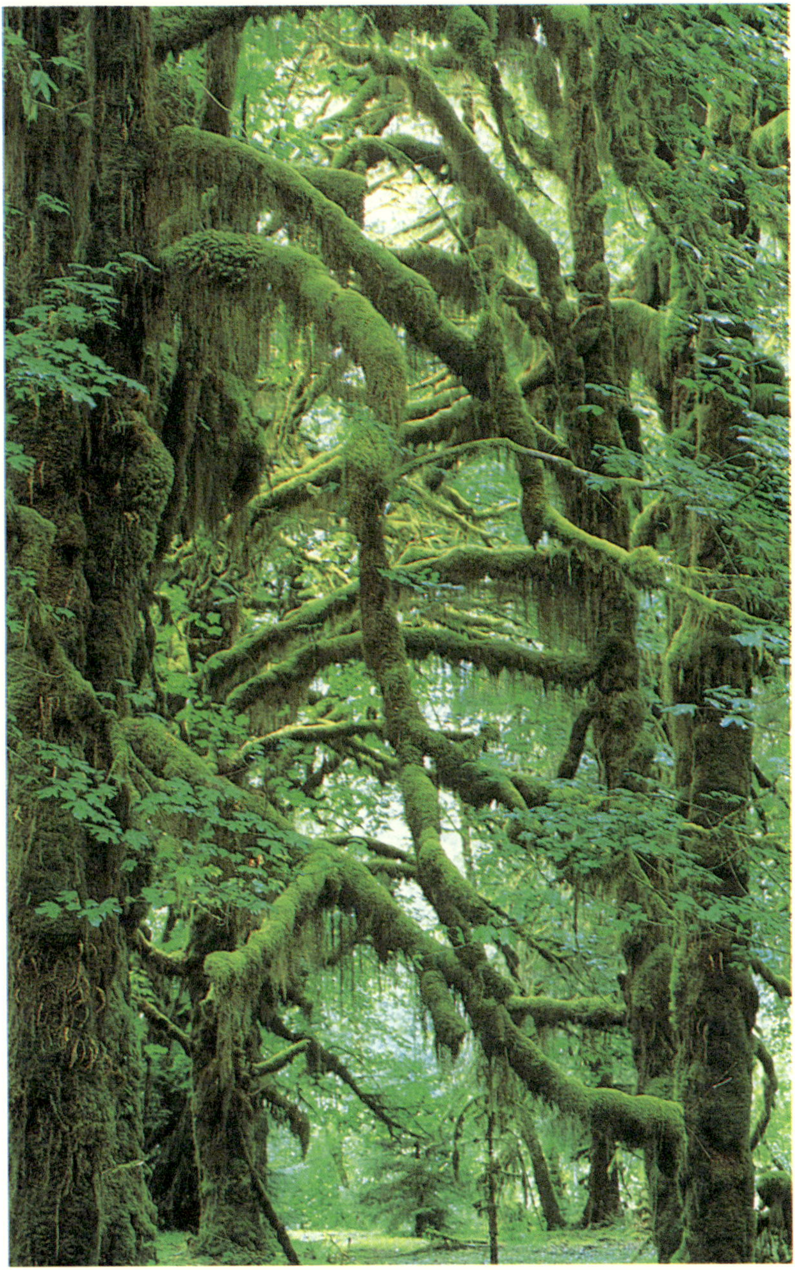

In all things,
God hates half-hearted attempts.

When enjoying yourself,
Doing it single-mindedly is the challenge.

If you go at a task half-heartedly,
The results will be poor.
Seek joy in days set afire with passion and enthusiasm.

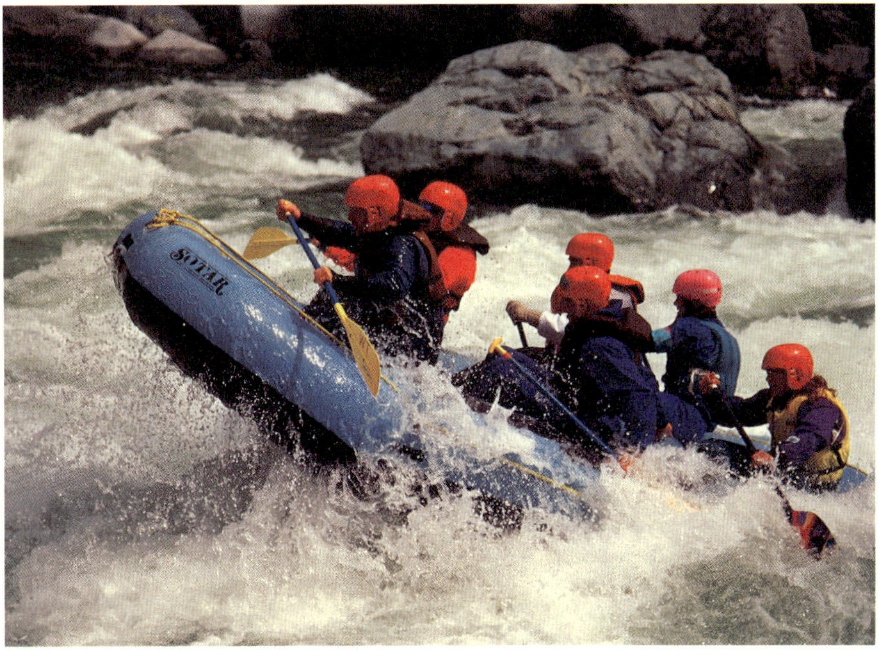
SOTAR

The most dangerous time is when
Nothing is going wrong,
Yet nothing is going right.
It is a warning.

Until it become wholly engaged in a task,
The soul sleeps.

The reason that things are not going well
Or that you seem unhappy
Is that your mind and body are not focused on doing
What they should be engaged in now.

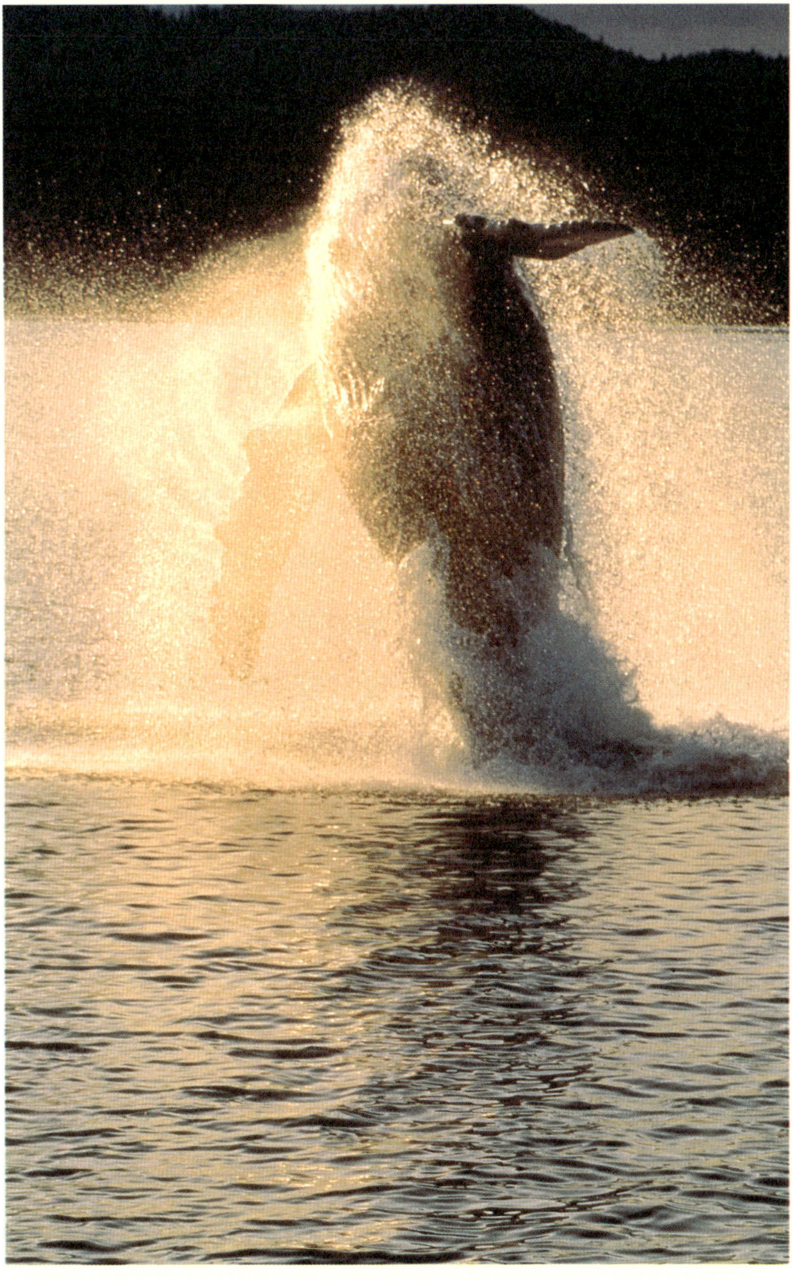

If you lack motivation,
Never assume that's just the way you are.
Sometimes unwanted feelings or emotions
Can hold you back on your path to growth.
But you can let go of those feelings
In a second
If you just choose to.

Unless you believe this,
You'll never be able to radically change yourself.

"He's not worth the effort."
"She's no good."

If you're a quitter,
That's most likely the way
People will end up thinking about you.

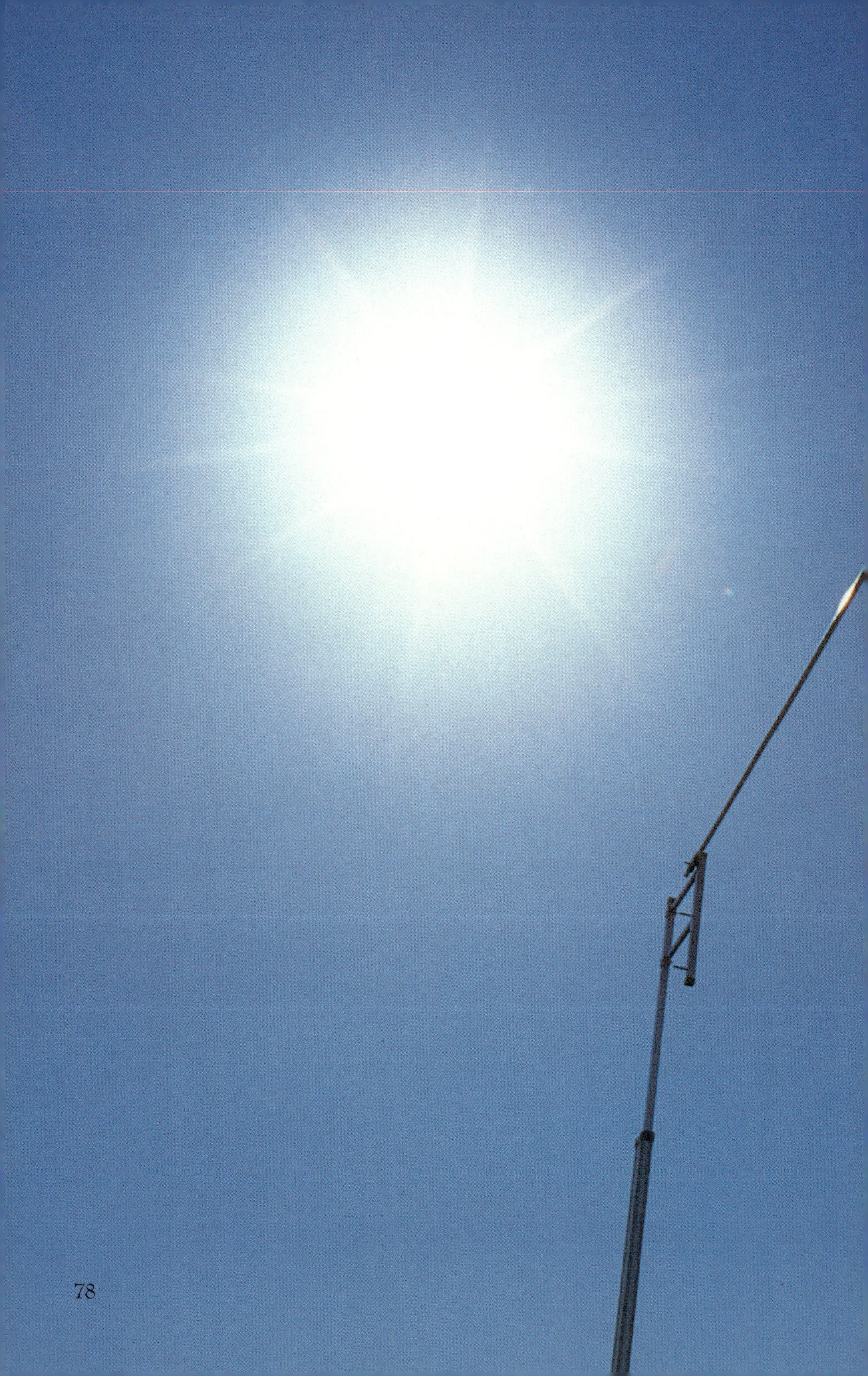

79

A careless man accomplishes little.

In all things, focused attention is critical.
What do you have to do to focus your attention?
All you have to do is start with something that interests you
And eventually you will find the way.

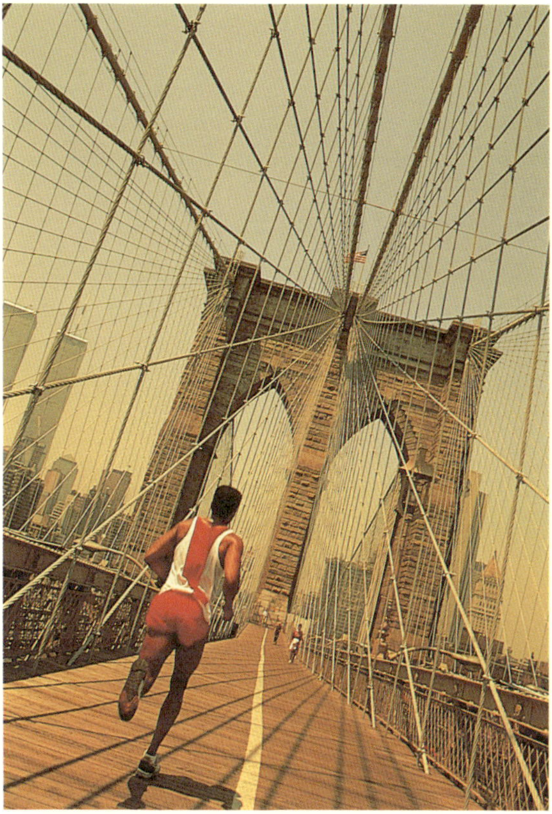

Don't think that you can accomplish things through effort alone.
Man is a self-centered being and believes that his every effort
Will be rewarded with success.

Effort alone isn't enough.
You need love.
You need sincerity.
You need a well-thought out plan.

Don't rely on people.
Overcome the difficulties in life with your own efforts
All the while relying on God.

Being timid will only invite harm.

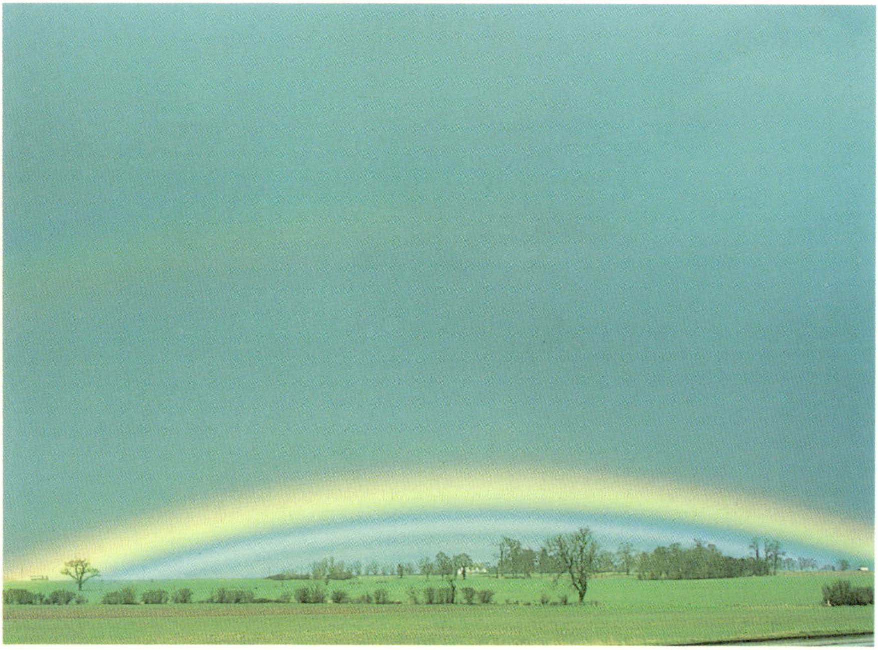

Be cautious but be undaunted.

One doesn't have to make a name for oneself;
Fame will come naturally on its own.

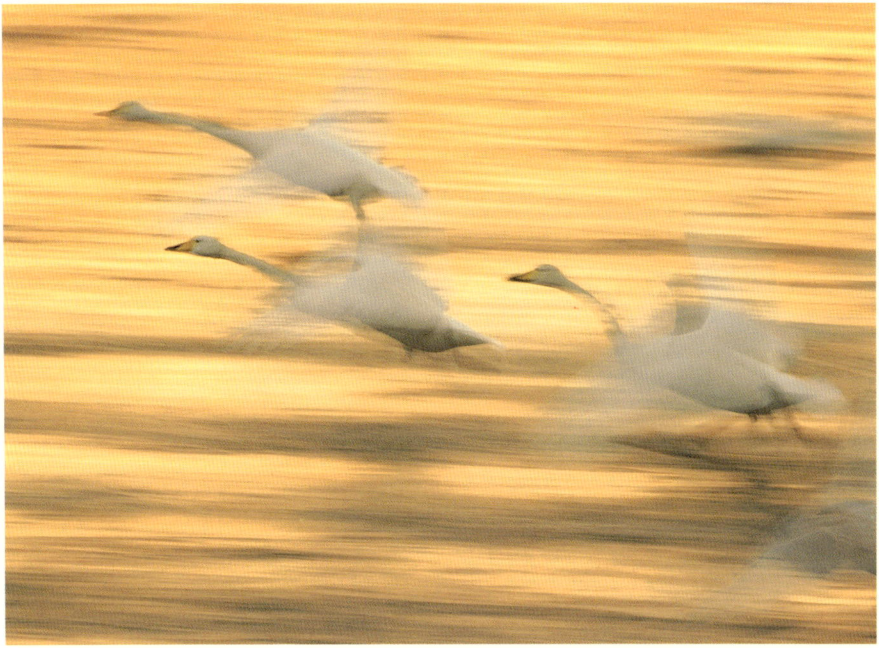

The reason a woman looks so beautiful
After giving birth to her first child
Is because her day is made full
by tasks which imitate God.

She warms milk so that it is easy for her child to drink.
She bathes her baby
And even when the infant wakes her crying in the night
She sees it merely as a sign of it being healthy
And the crying makes her baby all the more dear to her.

She worries if the baby's diaper is wet
Or whether the child might have a fever.

She forgets herself entirely,
Thinking only of another,
Her heart and soul are filled with loving thoughts.

Anyone who can act like that
To other people
And even to the things around them,
Is one with God.

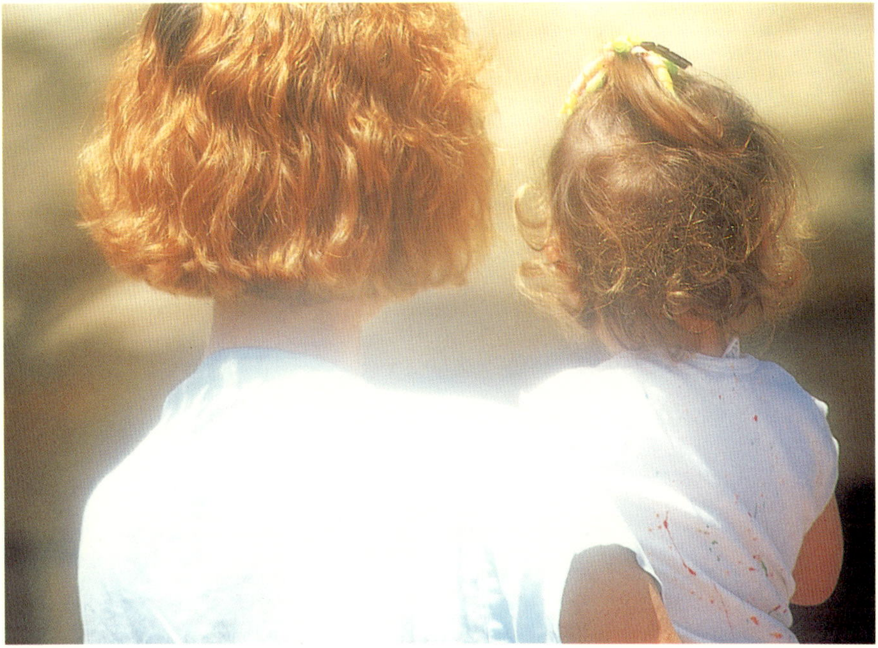

A longing to be cared for is a sign of having parents.
Look to be cared for not by people but by God.
See God as you father, God as your mother.

Simple and innocent people are the treasures of the world
Heaven delights in them and is pleased by their nature.

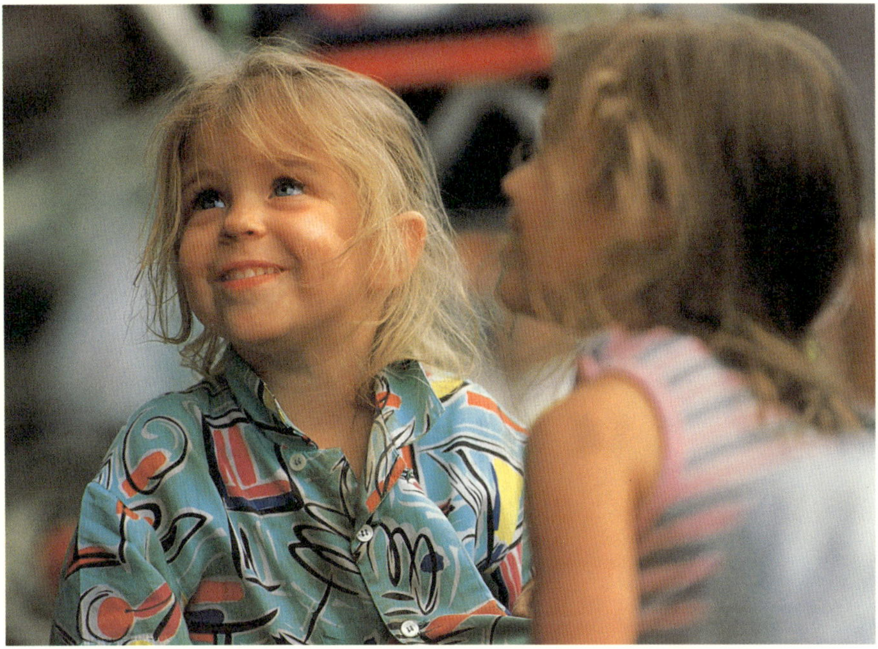

The only thing worse than having someone scold you
Is not having someone to scold you.

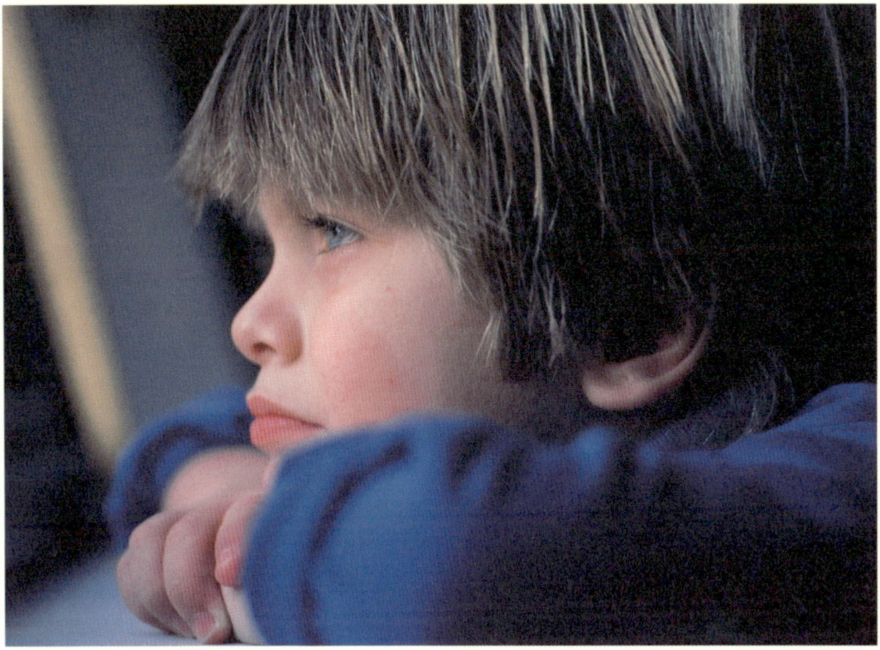

Be an artist, a religious thinker, a writer, and a philosopher
Who is also just an ordinary man.

Truly cosmopolitan people—
Men and women who see the world as small and inviting
Are like that.

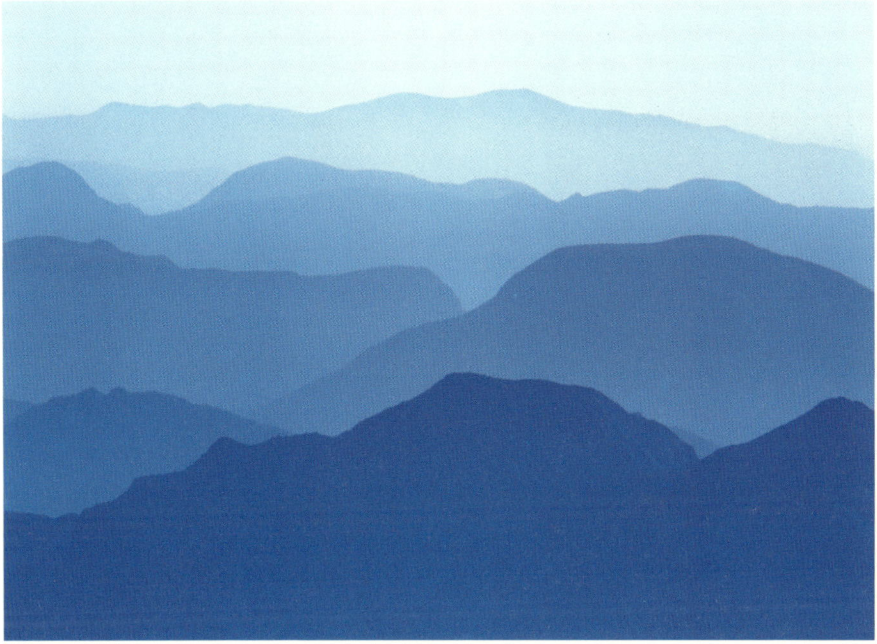

A great secret lies in how lightly you can speak of painful things
And how deeply you can speak of good things.

No matter how difficult things may be
If you are not afraid of death
Everything before you will appear calm.

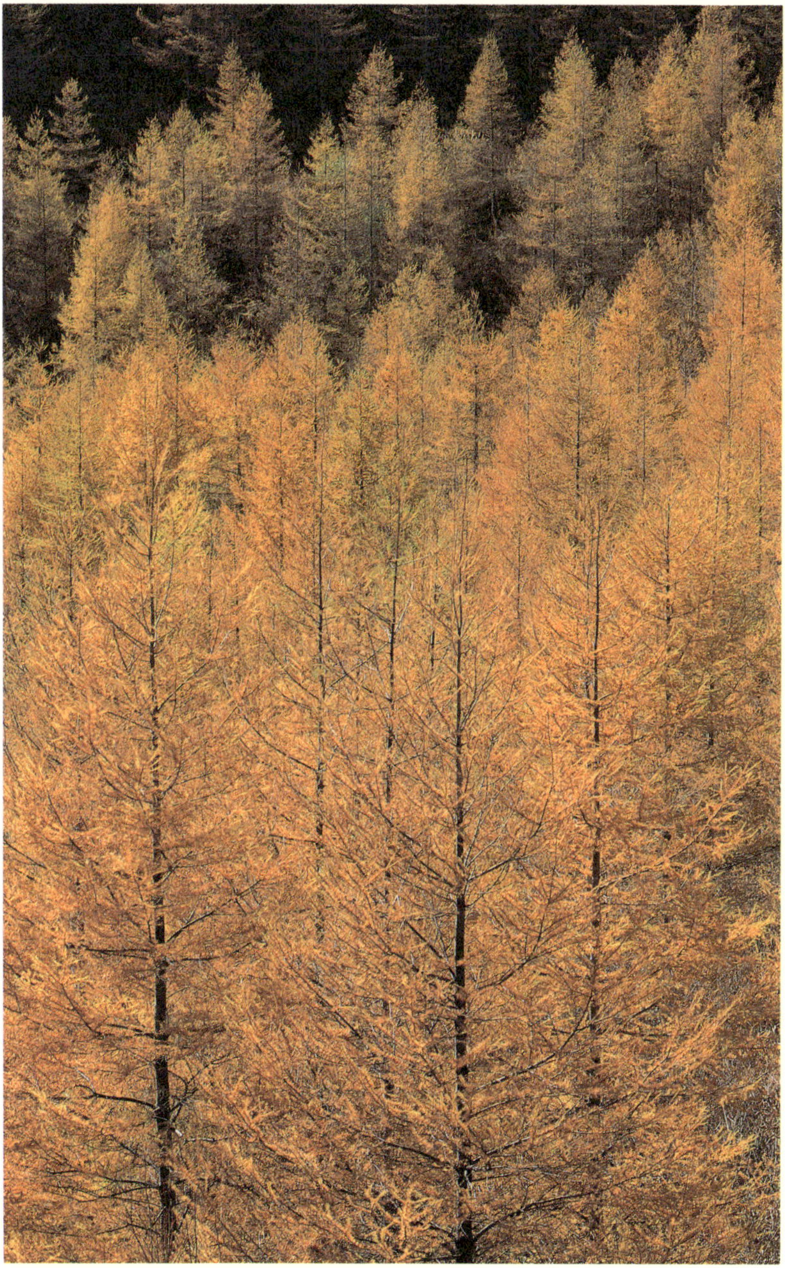

If you brace yourself for difficulties,
Difficulties will come your way.

Preoccupation with future problems
Will cause you to loose sight of the simple.

When God and Man are as one,
There is no longer room for illusion or facades.
And everything becomes simple, vibrant and alive.
The soul of Japan has seen this as a virtue,
One with the power to change people.

As for an age of peace,
It is an age when the spirit of Japan comes into full bloom.
It is an age of being pleased with God and delighting in Him.

Because there was little peace in the past,
there was competition and fighting.

Both man and God become genuine.

Spiritual awakening lies in knowing
That things worthy of being seen as wondrous
Are neither difficult nor remote.

The trick to living in the present
And strengthening the soul
Is to not look to the past
With thoughts of confronting what is already done.

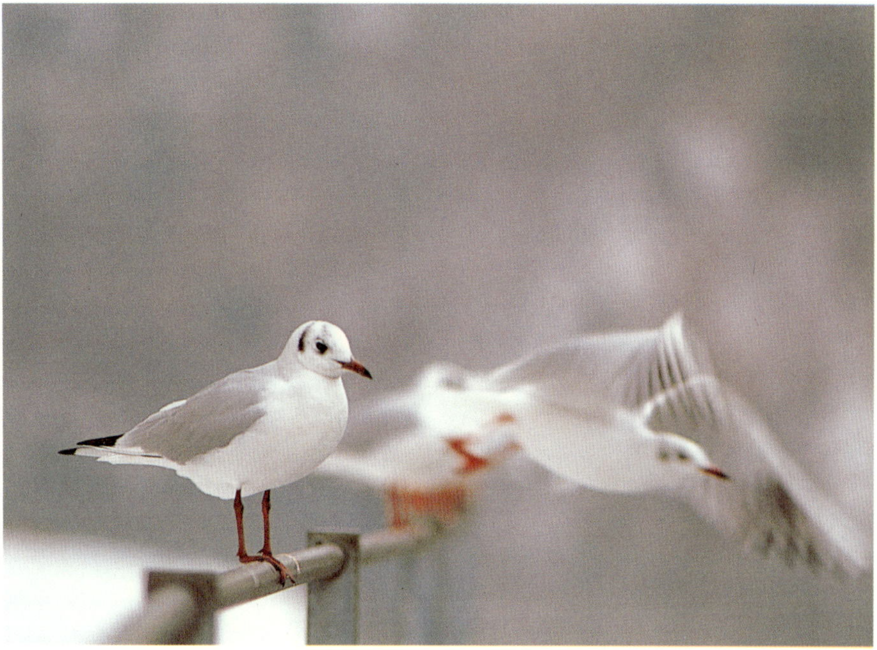

No one is a puppet.
Everyone is graced with a soul
Which dwells within them.

When you speak,
If you talk to people without speaking to their souls,
Then there's bound to be misunderstandings.

When you speak,
Imagine your soul
To be gently tumbling a gemstone
Within the soul of another.

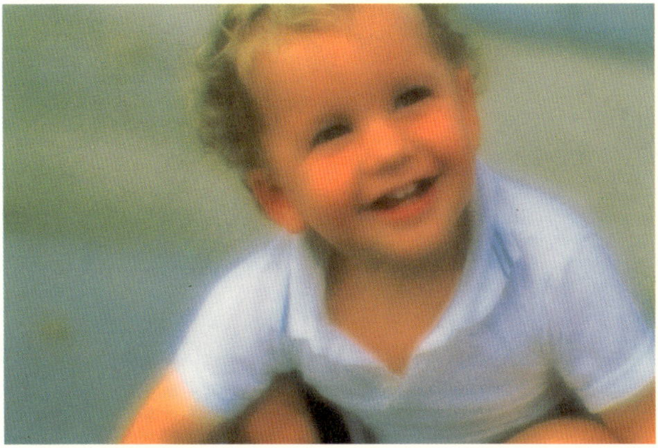

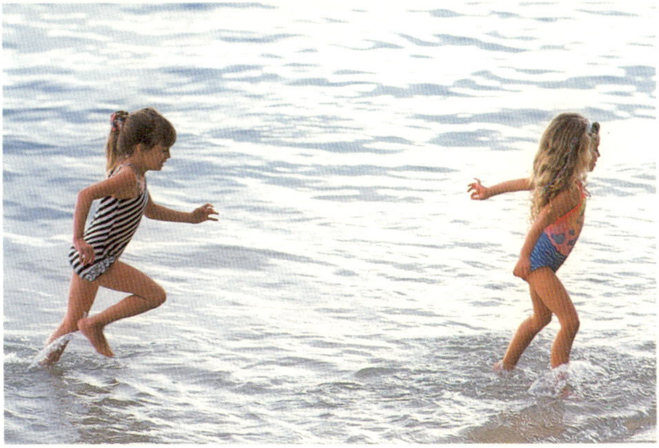

It is natural for people to want
To make a name for themselves.

However, as long as you hold that desire,
You won't be able to lead a life that pleases you.

God knows you.

And if one other special person knows you,
That's enough.

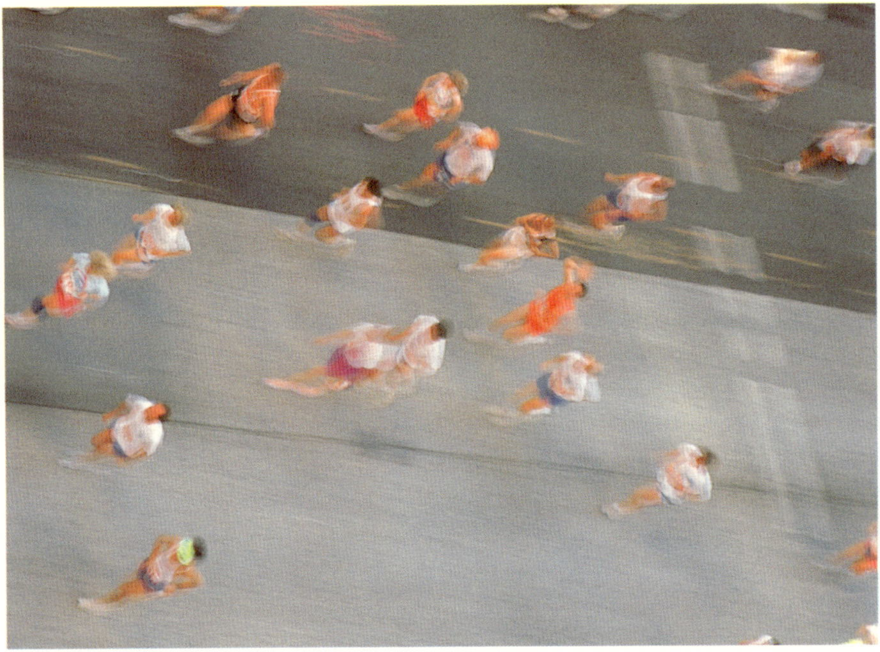

When hosting a banquet,
You need the effort and creativity
Of great supporters behind the scenes.

People who work out of the spotlight
Truly are working to be close to God.

Those who can discern their efforts,
Are those who have perfected Love.

Carrefour Nice
Carrefour Nice
Carrefour Nice
Carrefour Nice

Spiritual training can be done
Without people realizing it.

Evil can be done without people knowing it.
Yet God sees all.

The existence of blessings and judgment
Is the mechanism of Divine Fairness.

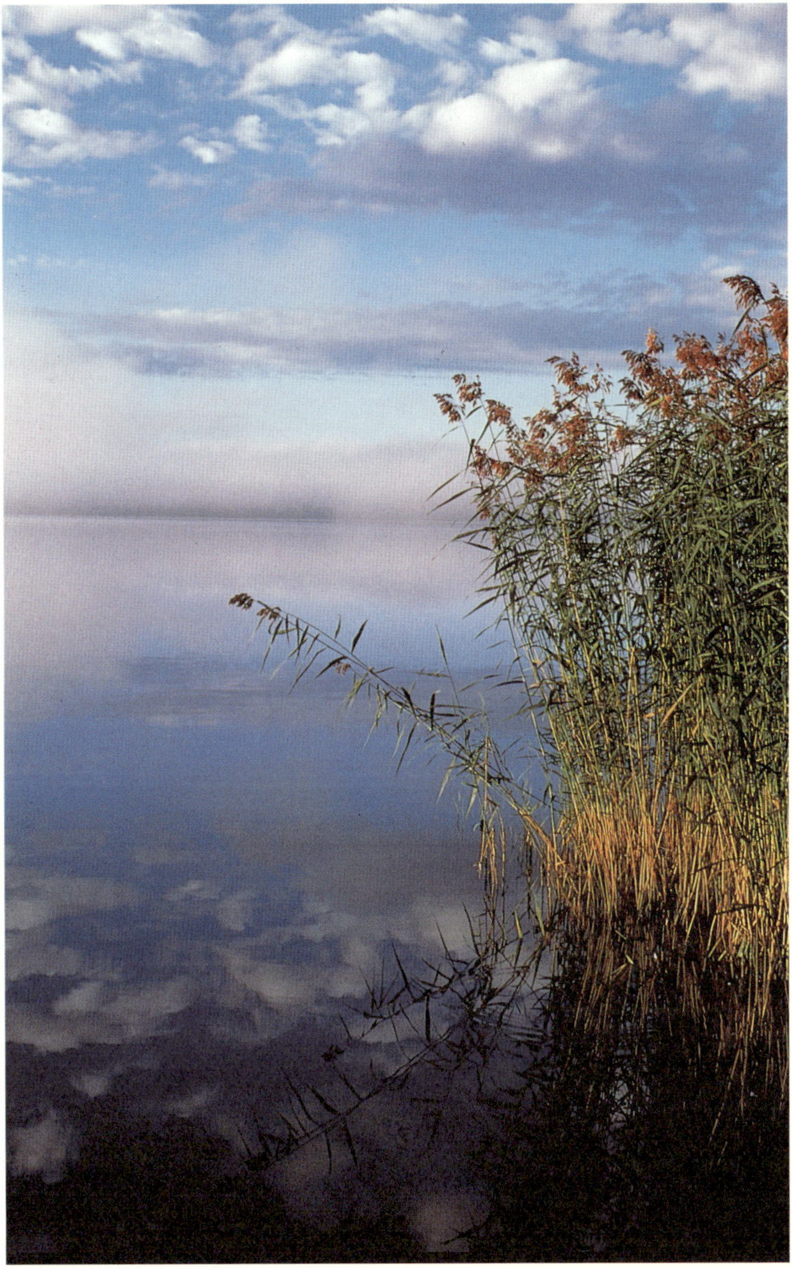

Realize that
The people that we meet and part from in life
Are sent at the direction of Heaven and Earth.

Don't search for treasure.
It will be given to you in measure
Commensurate with your virtue and strength.

Even though it seems like you've polished your soul,
There still is room for greater development.

Look to the future and develop yourself.
Train yourself to pay attention to the little things in life.
Train yourself to be able to gain the trust of others.
Train yourself to calmly make the right decisions
Without being swayed by what others think.

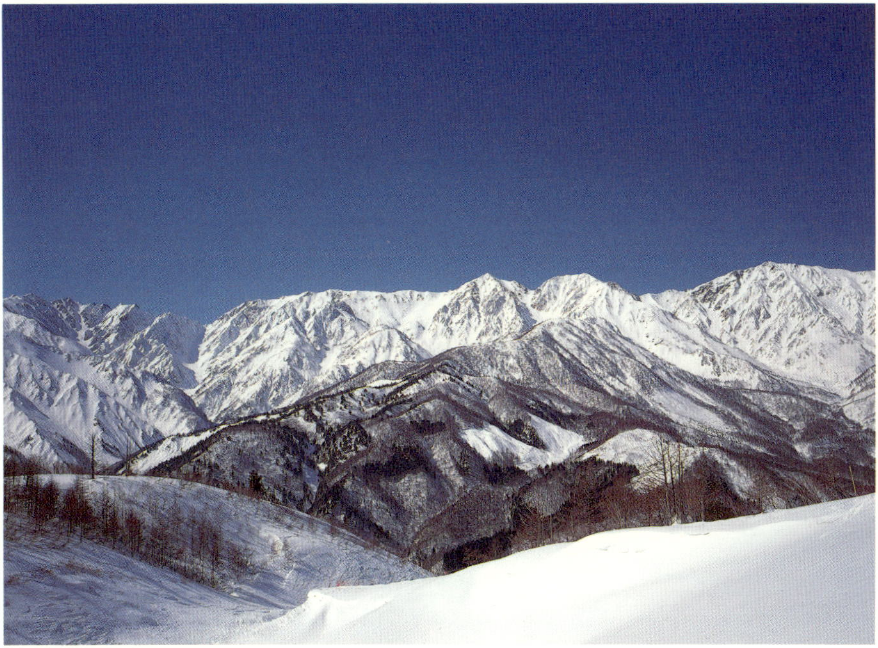

People who are thoroughly enlightened
Have stripped away the masks of their own egos
One by one.

Developing people who can discipline themselves
Is the goal of education.

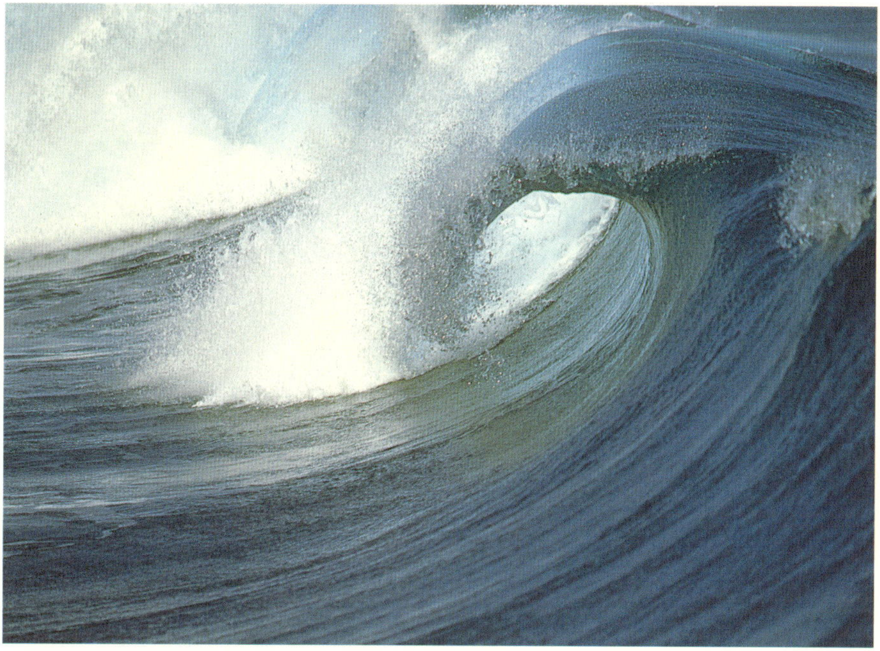

Endurance is progress.

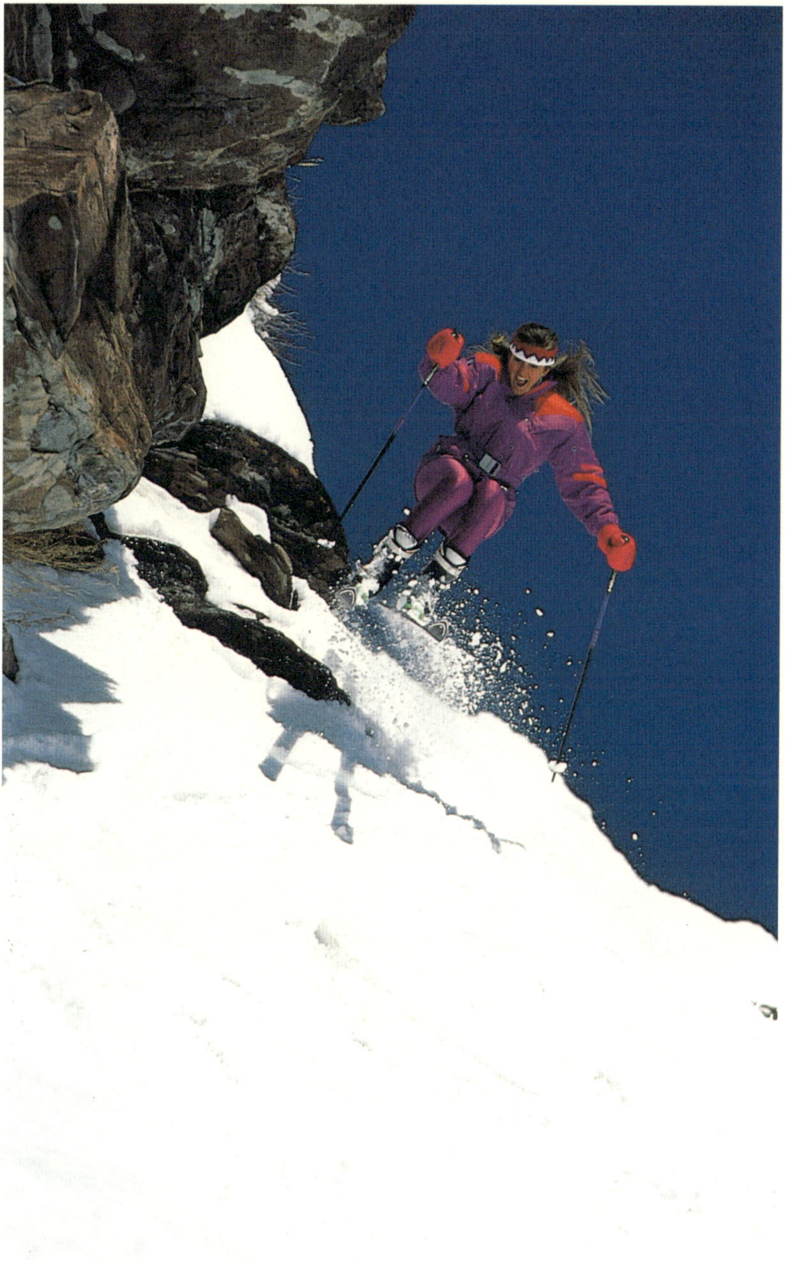

Without the attitude that
You'll go on even if you're the last person on earth,
You'll never be a leader.

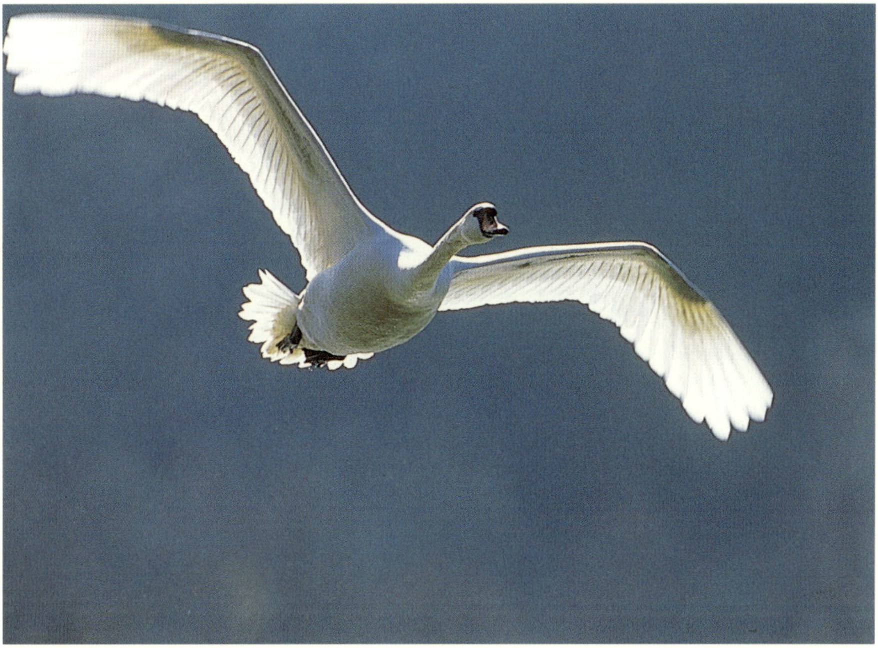

Perfecting your soul consists of
Disciplining your thoughts in everyday life.
The spiritual path
Consists of filling your mind solely
With gratitude and the desire for self-improvement.
There is nothing else
Worthy of the name of spiritual training.

Other self-denials and trials are
At best,
Ways to broaden yourself.
At worst,
Mere spiritual embellishments.

In and of themselves,
There is nothing in these denials
To be proud of.
What one self-importantly believes
To be spiritual suffering,
Is perhaps in reality
Little more than one's own ego
Coming in conflict with the egos of others.

The cause of this suffering is illusion.

So, begin changing the way you view things
And in doing so work through your karma
Through the activities of your everyday life.

There is nothing you need to do but
Continue to strive and live fully in the moment.

Such is a life will truly polish the soul.

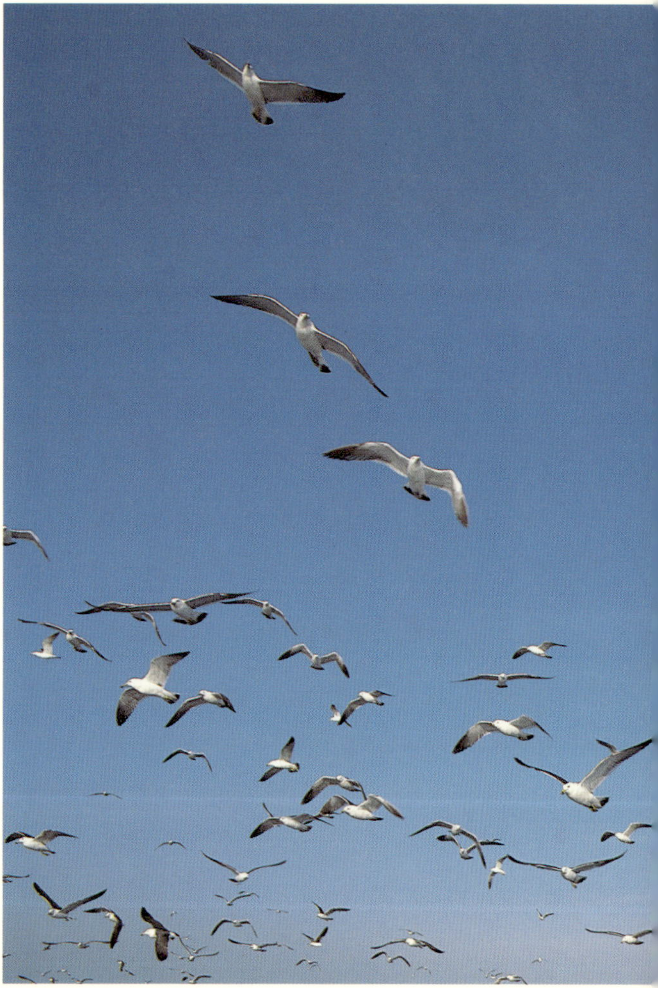

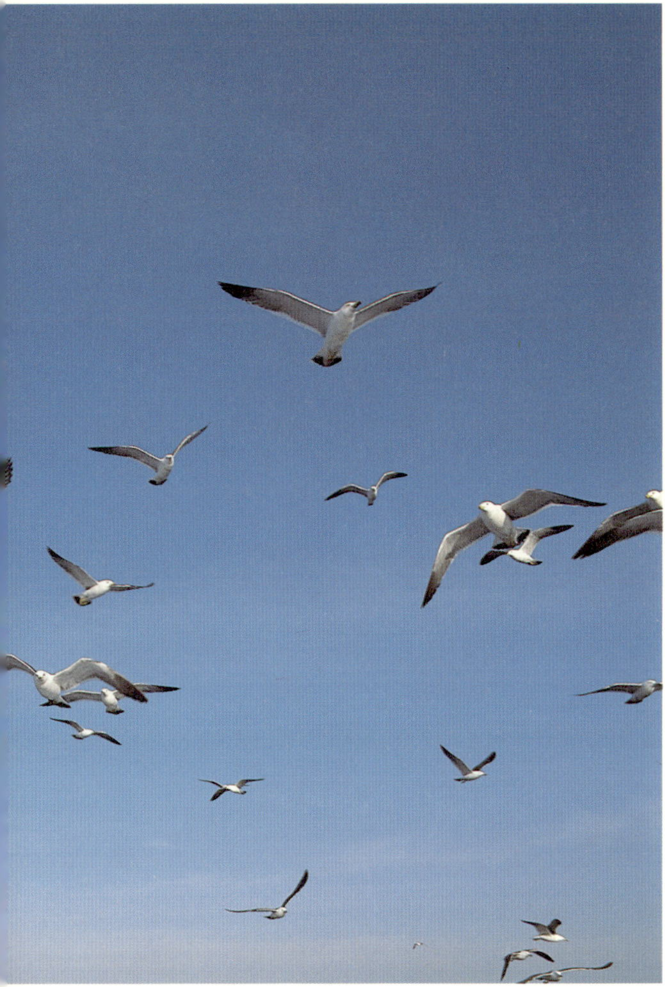

Take a few steps forward and stop,
Take a few more and stop.

Carefully nurture each and every seed.
Harvest them and then plant the next seeds.

This also is the cycle for increasing
The fruits of one's faith.

A person's life cannot be measured by human standards.
A life is an ongoing individual act of creation.

The individual is like the phoenix.

Like the phoenix,
People seeking the Sixth Realm
Rise unmarred by the trials of life,

With wings outstretched,
They soar through the sky toward the sun.

The perfect symbol of the unblemished soul.

Profile

Toshu Fukami (Haruhisa Handa)

Toshu Fukami, officially known as Haruhisa Handa, was born in 1951. He graduated from Doshisha University with a degree in economics. After completing a master class in vocal music at the Musashino Academia Musicae, he went on to earn a master's degree in creative arts from the Western Australian Academy of Performing Arts (WAAPA) at Edith Cowan University in Australia and a Ph.D. in literature from the Academy of Arts and Design, Tsinghua University. He also earned a second Ph.D. in classical Chinese literature from Zhejiang University. Fukami serves as chancellor and professor of international politics in the College of Social Sciences at the University of Cambodia. He is senior international commentator for Southeast Asia Television and Radio and senior editorial writer at *Southeast Asia Weekly*. He also holds professorships at Ariake College of Education and the Arts (music) and the Institute for Japanese Culture Studies, Zhejiang Gongshang University in China, and also holds positions at several other universities in the UK and China. He was awarded an honorary degree of Doctor of Humane Letters from the Juilliard School and is an honorary fellow at Corpus Christi College, University of Oxford and the School of Oriental and African Studies (SOAS) at London University. He serves as an adviser to the Royal Government of Cambodia with the rank of minister, as advisor to the Prime Minister of the Kingdom of Cambodia, and as honorary consul of the Kingdom of Cambodia in Fukuoka.

Fukami was accredited by the Chinese government as First Grade National Master of Fine Arts, First Grade National Opera Singer and Second Grade National Peking Opera Actor. He belongs to National Chinese Opera and Dance Drama Company. He is also a Noh performer, belonging to the Hosho School, and member of the Noh Association. Fukami is a member of the Japan P.E.N. Club and member of the Modern Haiku Association. He is the leader of World Mate. In the golf world, Fukami serves as chairman of the Legends Tour (Women's Senior Golf Association) of the United States, honorary lifetime member of the PGA of Australia, patron of Golf Australia, which is comparable to Japan Golf Association (JGA), and honorary president of the International Blind Golf Association. He is a master of calligraphy, the Japanese tea ceremony and of Japanese flower arrangement. Fukami has also produced opera, plays, and Takigi Noh (open-air Noh) and has performed as the leading role. His calligraphy is part of the permanent collection of the British Museum. His paintings are part of the permanent collection of the Chinese National Academy of Arts. Fukami has written over 270 books covering a vast range of topics from collections of side-splitting gags, academic articles, haiku poems, collections of his own art works, cooking books, spiritual books, books on business know-how, etc. In addition he is widely known as a radio and TV personality and commentator and has had many regular shows. He appears regularly in the TV program, "Success Toryumon (Gateway to Success)."